Thicker Than Water?

Thicker Than Water?

Adoption:
its loyalties, pitfalls and joys

ALICE HEIM

Secker & Warburg

London

First published in England 1983 by
Martin Secker & Warburg Limited
54 Poland Street, London W1V 3DF

The extract from *The Times* article, 11 June 1981, that appears on pages 104–
is reproduced by kind permission of Times Newspapers Ltd.
The extract from *Up in the Clouds, Gentlemen Please* by Sir John Mills that
appears on page 184 is reproduced by kind permission of Weidenfeld &
Nicolson Ltd.

British Library Cataloguing in Publication Data

Heim, Alice
    Thicker than water?
    1. Adoption
    I. Title   36.7,34   HV875
Cloth ISBN 0-436-19155-5
Paperback ISBN 0-436-19156-3

Set in Great Britain by Bookens, Saffron Walden, Essex

Printed in Great Britain by
Biddles Limited, Guildford & King's Lynn

To my grandchildren,
Maria and Robert

Contents

Acknowledgments

I am indebted to many people for valuable criticism. In particular, I wish to express thanks to Dr Margaret Wallace and Dr Jane Robson for their comments on the chapters on the Facts of Life and on Illnesses and Accidents; to Nancy Harris for her helpful additions; and to Patrick Wilkinson, Hester Hinde and Peter Dallas-Smith for their acute, yet kindly, recognition of unacceptable modes of expression.

My gratitude goes too to the parents who contributed to the chapter on Conversations with Jo; and, above all, to the adoptees and adoptive parents who had the courage and understanding to produce their narratives.

A.W.H.
January 1983

Introduction

When, long ago, my Publishers suggested that I should write a book on bringing up adopted children, my daughter and son were in their mid-teens. I said, "But bringing up adopted children is just like bringing up one's biologically own children." "That," came the reply, "is why *you* must write it."

I think that in one sense I was right, or rather I have not changed my mind during the intervening years. My views on methods of upbringing have been confirmed by my own experience and (both positively and negatively) by the experiences of friends and acquaintances with their children and grandchildren. These views are given in Part II of this book – which deals with the upbringing of children from infancy to adulthood – and applies equally to adopted and to "biological" offspring. I use the term "biological" to signify sons and daughters born to their parents. This is in preference to the word "natural", which is often used simply to denote illegitimacy; and in preference to the phrase "their own offspring" since adoptive parents feel, understandably and intensely, that their children are very much their own.

In another sense, however, I was mistaken in my statement that bringing up adoptees is just like bringing up "biological" offspring. Problems do sometimes arise in the case of adoption, stemming directly from the fact of adoption, and it is these problems that are dealt with in Part I. It is not always easy to distinguish the problems "stemming directly from the fact of adoption" from those which would have arisen in any case, owing to the relationship between the generations or to external circumstances. We all know, alas, of biological children who have become psychologically disturbed, or

1

alienated from their parents, who have committed suicide, who have dropped out, who have become addicted to drugs or alcohol or a life of crime. Although this can and does happen also with adoptees it is evidently unlikely, in most cases, to be *due to* adoption.

I have tried, therefore, in the chapters that follow to confine myself to difficulties which may arise specifically from the adoption situation. But I am well aware that the distinction is not clear-cut. My method has been to send a circular letter to all the adult adoptees whom I was able to discover, and another circular letter to all the adoptive parents whom I could find. Copies of both these letters are to be found at the end of the chapter.

Some of my advisers have been so acutely conscious of the arbitrariness of this approach that they have suggested that I should use a "control group" as well as a "main group", that is, that I should send similar, but suitably re-worded, letters to biological parents and to the offspring born to them – if the latter were over sixteen years of age. Discussion of this proposal, however, usually ended in mirth! How can one expect people to think up problems arising as a result of their having been born to, and brought up by, their parents?

There is, of course, a further element of arbitrariness in the method used, in that most of the recipients were either friends of mine (whom I requested to forward the letter to anyone appropriate they knew) or friends of friends. I tried to cast the net as widely as possible by invoking the aid also of one or two schools – though I did not achieve many contributors in this way. And people professionally engaged in adoption, such as social workers and adoption officers, were understandably reluctant to get involved, feeling that their integrity and the guarantee of confidentiality might be questioned (despite my own promise of ensuring that nobody quoted in the book would be identifiable).

Finally, there is the inevitable self-selection inherent in any such enterprise. I sent out over a hundred letters to adoptive parents and roughly the same number to Dear Unknown (see below). In the event, well under half responded; and of those parents who did reply, a few declined to answer my queries and to pass on the relevant letter to their adopted sons and daughters. Such answers tended to take the following form:

> "All is well with us and our two adopted sons – now grown-up and married – but we do not wish to stir anything up."

"I am so sorry to be so long answering your letter and even more sorry not to be able to help. I have given the project considerable thought. There are some personal reasons for my not being able to pass on your paper to my son: pretty deep-rooted reasons. And in addition, he is engaged now in making a big change of work, and on the move, and I have doubts that he will, in fact, write to you the details you would like to have." [Of course he did not do so, since he never saw the letter. Note the slight confusion of thought here – probably induced by intense feeling, in an otherwise clear-headed writer.]

"I have become increasingly uneasy as to whether I could ask my daughters to help as you suggested. Probably had the request for information been in the more conventional form of a questionnaire, their reaction might have been more predictable: but I feel that the open-ended questions which the letter puts before them might have both worried and disturbed them – and one especially might have preferred that this particular sleeping dog should have been left comfortably asleep . . . Both are happily married, with children they enjoy; and they are very friendly, confiding in each other and asking each other for advice. And our relationship with them is affectionate and relaxed, so you may wonder why I am reluctant to ask them. I can only say that I have an intuitive feeling that it *might* be better not to."

Several other parents and adoptees commented unfavourably on the open-ended form of my two circular letters. It was quite deliberate on my part since I wished to avoid leading or loaded questions, and wanted my correspondents to decide for themselves which aspects of adoption seemed to them most significant. As will be seen in later chapters, this approach proved very fruitful in the case of people who did feel able to respond. Only two of the forty-odd who co-operated replied anonymously – despite the invitation to do so, should they prefer this. It seems to me a token of good faith that all the others elected to give their names and addresses. Many of those who responded positively gave also their telephone number and invited me to ring them up or to go to see them, should I so desire.

I will give one further example of my drawing a blank, this time from a middle-aged (married) adopted daughter who was described, by a third party, as a trouble-maker who had severed all relations with her adoptive family. She wrote (to the third party): "I imagine you are aware that I do not have any contact with Bristol any more which, needless to say, is a great sadness to James and me. So I do not think it would be appropriate or beneficial to anybody for me to dredge up the past again."

In the last quotation and in all others in this book, place-names and people's names have been altered, to render the cases unrecognisable. The sex of the adoptee, his/her present age and marital status, and the age at adoption are, however, correctly stated where known.

The above illustrations might suggest that my respondents were unrepresentative in two respects: (a) That they were all well-educated and highly intelligent, and (b) that in general only the "successes" felt able to co-operate. With regard to (a), not all were so strikingly literate: I received a few replies which were poorly expressed, confused and ill-spelt. These do form a rather small minority – unfortunately from the viewpoint of getting a representative sample. Where I quote from such letters, I have corrected the English and spelling – while in no way altering the meaning.

With regard to (b), it is certainly not the case that replies came only from "successful" parents and adoptees. If the criteria for success are to be taken as fulfilment of the adoptee's emotional and intellectual potential – whatever this may be – then it is clear from many of the quotations from respondents, given in subsequent chapters, that by no means all were successful. Indeed, I gained the impression from certain letters that some of the writers welcomed the opportunity of getting off their chests long-held grudges – secure in the knowledge that they were writing to someone who did not know them and that their own identity would remain unrevealed.

Copy of circular letter for adult adoptees

Dear Unknown,

I am writing a book on bringing up adopted children. I, myself, have a daughter and a son, now in their twenties, whom I adopted when they were a few weeks old. My writing will stem largely from my own experience, but I do realise that two is rather a small sample on which to base a book! I realise also that the book would be incomplete without including the viewpoint of *the adoptee*: hence this letter.

I am writing to all the people I can find who were adopted, asking them to help me in this piece of research. If you are willing to co-operate, would you be so kind as to write down all the

4

advantages and the drawbacks that you have encountered, as a result of being adopted. If you would care to add any other relevant information this would be most welcome.

I shall naturally treat all replies as strictly confidential. I shall not mention the name of any of my correspondents and shall ensure that no reader of the book will be able to identify anybody. Indeed, if you prefer to withhold your name, it is not essential for me to know it. But I should like to know, please, your present age, your age when adopted, and your sex and also whether you were brought up with any brothers and sisters – either adopted, or the biological children of your adoptive parents.

I enclose an extra copy of this letter, in case you know of any other adopted person who might be prepared to help. In that event, would you please hand on to them the second copy. I shall gladly let you have further copies if you know of several possible helpers.

I shall be very grateful if you do feel able to co-operate. If so, would you be kind enough to let me have your answer within a month or two? – definitely before the end of February, 1980.

Yours sincerely

After I had sent out quite a few copies of this letter, I was approached by several adoptive parents – some of whom knew me personally and some of whom did not – with the request they they too should be enabled to present their point of view. I therefore produced:

Circular letter II – for adoptive parents

Dear Adoptive Parents,
You may have heard that I am writing a book on Bringing Up Adopted Children. Indeed, you may already have seen my circular letter, which begins DEAR UNKNOWN and is addressed to adults who were adopted in infancy or early childhood.

In that letter I explained that I have, myself, an adopted son and daughter – now in their early 20s, adopted when they were a few weeks old. I asked the adopt*ees* to let me know, in strictest confidence, what they regarded as the advantages and the drawbacks of being adopted.

I should like, now, to get the viewpoint of the adopt*ers*: hence this letter. I should be exceedingly grateful if you would be kind enough to let me have some notes on your experience as adoptive parents – written jointly or separately. In particular I should welcome information concerning any problems that have arisen, directly or indirectly as a result of your sons/daughters having been adopted.

All relevant information, however, will be gratefully accepted. And all communications will of course be treated strictly confidentially. No names will be revealed in the book and nobody will be identifiable. Indeed, if you prefer to withhold your name, I do not need to have it. But I should like to know, please, how many children you adopted; their present age(s) and their age(s) when adopted; and whether you had, in addition, any children biologically your own.

In case you prefer to withhold your address, may I take the opportunity now of thanking you for your co-operation – if you do decide to help me in my research. I shall be very grateful indeed if you decide to do so.

Yours sincerely

PART ONE

I

The Adoptee's Viewpoint:
Advantages

The adoptees who answered my letter ranged in age from late teens to late fifties, roughly equal numbers of men and women electing to reply. Some firmly adhered to the wording of my letter, responding mainly in terms of the advantages and drawbacks of adoption, as they saw it. Of these, one (Susan Oak, in her early twenties, adopted at six weeks) wrote uncompromisingly that "to be adopted has no disadvantages. If anything it is assured of having at least one advantage in that at least the adopted child is wanted by his or her adoptive parents."

Another respondent (Michael Elm, early fifties, adopted at four and a half years of age) replied equally positively that there are "no advantages in adoption, rather the reverse". Mr Elm had a sister, adopted as a two-year old, some two years after his adoption. "If anything," he wrote, "her fate was even worse than mine." As she had died some years before I embarked on this search, I was unable to get her point of view. But Mr Elm added that he himself is happily married, with two teenage children of whom he is very fond and proud. I attempted but failed to elicit from him what his specific difficulties had been, in childhood and adolescence.

Most of my replies were mixed, containing a blend of satisfactions and dissatisfactions – as I imagine would be the case in a study of biological families. But one cause for deep satisfaction was repeatedly mentioned, by men and women, young and middle-aged, regardless of their age at adoption, namely the fact that they were much wanted by their adoptive parents. Thus Tony Pine, adopted at a few weeks, now in his early thirties and married, wrote: "A strong point I have always felt in favour of being an adopted child is that you know definitely that you were wanted very badly by your adoptive parents. Otherwise they would not have gone through all the rigmarole to get me. Or at least, I would never think that my adoptive parents had got me by accident (though my natural ones very probably did!)"

Mrs Kate Poplar, now in her early thirties, was adopted at fourteen months. She writes: "I have thought about the advantages of being adopted and I think the most important one was the feeling that you were really 'wanted' by your adoptive parents." Robert Ash, adopted at six months, now in his late forties and married, used exactly the same phrase.

Margaret Beech was adopted at six weeks by an unmarried woman of about forty years of age. Margaret writes: "What gave me a special glow for many years was the feeling that I was specially selected from lots of other babies!" This leads on to a further possible advantage for adoptees, namely the belief that they have been individually chosen, as opposed to children born to their parents – who just accept whatever offspring come their way! Thus a number of my respondents wrote that they were "specially chosen", or at least that their adoptive parents had told them, when explaining about adoption, that they were specially chosen. A few related that they used to be read to from a book called *The Chosen Child* – which became a great favourite with them.

Evidently this statement can give adoptees a lot of pleasure and reassurance in early childhood – though they may become somewhat sceptical and questioning at a later date as to the mechanism of the selection process. For this reason I did not ever tell my adopted son and daughter that they were "chosen", although I had told them from the very beginning – long before this could have any meaning for them – that they were adopted. But one day, when they were respectively six and seven years old, and I was feeling particularly affectionate and grateful for their existence, I said: "Isn't it funny, there are so many children in the world, but of all the possible children you two are the ones I'd always have loved the most" – whereupon my son said thoughtfully: "But you wouldn't have *known*, would you?"

Another advantage claimed by some of my correspondents was the chance of fantasising about their origins afforded by the fact of being adopted. (Such fantasies are not uncommon also in biological children, but evidently this fact did not occur to the adoptees who wrote about them.) For instance, Mrs Jane Hawthorn, who was adopted at six weeks, writes: "The adopted child may have many fantasies as to who their parents are, which is not open to natural children." But she goes on to say that "Accompanying the thoughts are ones of guilt because of the gratitude and debt owed to the parents who brought one up and the fear of hurting their feelings if one makes too many enquiries."

For Richard Plane, however, "The possibility that I am the illegitimate son of a famous family cannot be ruled out." Whilst the adoptive mother of Janet Birch wrote: "I discovered through the mother of a young school-friend that Janet had been shooting a line at school that she might be the daughter of a princess. The school-friend was very envious and complained to her mother that she wished her origins were more exalted. I thought this little bit of fantasy was rather delightful and very typical of a little girl (who was about eleven at the time). I can't see a little boy wishing he were the son of a prince."

A number of more practical advantages were recognised by adoptees who compared their (adoptive) circumstances with the circumstances they imagined would have been theirs, had they not been adopted. Thus Mrs Ruth Willow (late forties, adopted at two and a half years), wrote: "I was brought up in a family versus in a 'Home' where Mother kept me"; and this had the advantage of providing "a father figure, therefore outwardly an acceptable 'normal' family". Several adoptees commented on their preference for living in a family as opposed to an institution.

Mrs Pauline Whitebeam (early forties, adopted at six weeks) wrote in a delightfully matter-of-fact way: "My brother was also adopted at six weeks. He is thirty-nine now and we were brought up together as brother and sister (he is not from the same original parents as myself) and we were told of our adoption when we were about seven years old. That's a long time ago now! But I cannot remember it having any effect, bad or otherwise, on my relationship with my parents. To me my Mum and Dad have always been that, and only on very rare occasions can I remember wondering about my actual parents, but I do sometimes wonder if I have any true brothers or sisters as I am a very gregarious person, but I have never felt strongly enough about it to start a search. I have never shrugged from mentioning my adoption when asked questions on my family history (e.g., when I was pregnant). I am married and we have two boys of our own now."

A number of my correspondents, however, seem to feel in a more absolute way that they are positively glad to have been adopted – not just in comparison with the institutional upbringing that they might have had, but in comparison with the more usual, biological family. George Sycamore, for instance (adopted at six months by a single woman – no blood relationship – now in his early fifties, married) illustrates this attitude very vividly: "It made me feel proud and special . . . I think there is a physical, emotional bond between [biological] mother and child that gets in the way of logical, reasoned and planned upbringing . . . I was spared the conflict between parents which some children have to suffer." And again, "Not being a blood relation did help with any friction with the uncles and aunts, and especially with the cousins. I knew I was different from them, and not being a blood relation explained the difference and was a let-out for me in my own mind."

This impression of George's is interesting and it appeared, in various guises, in several letters: the feeling experienced by some adoptees that they are allowed to be more essentially *themselves* than are biological offspring – as though the latter get moulded in accordance with the expectations of their family who, with hindsight, know all about them in advance. One of my two anonymous contributors informed me that he was male, nineteen years of age, adopted when a few months old and had a "considerably older sister, the natural daughter of my adoptive parents". Let us call him Edward Coppice. He wrote: "I would just like to mention an aspect of being adopted that is rather important to me – though I hope not in too self-conscious a way. That is what I have come to think of as the liberating force of independence in individuals, independence that is, in one's own development and growth. So that I have found myself in a certain beneficial – because responsible – way an 'outsider' whilst remaining in every sense part of a family."

Thus for George Sycamore and Edward Coppice, the fact of being brought up by adoptive parents confers an intrinsic benefit. But, as will be seen in the next chapter, lack of blood relatives among the older generation is sometimes felt by an adoptee to be, on the contrary, a serious deficiency.

II
The Adoptee's Viewpoint: Drawbacks

In this chapter I discuss the drawbacks of adoption, again as perceived by the adoptee. It will be seen that this chapter is rather longer than the preceding one: that the number of disadvantages cited exceeds the number of advantages. If this conveys the impression that drawbacks are in general felt by the adoptee to outweigh advantages, this would be highly misleading. The advantages outlined in Chapter I were mentioned again and again by different correspondents, whereas many of the drawbacks given below were described by one and only one adoptee. That is, the disadvantages cited were more *varied* than the assets. The opening words of *Anna Karenina* irresistibly spring to mind: "All happy families resemble one another, every unhappy family is unhappy after its own fashion."

Let us begin with the question of blood relationship since this was raised at the end of the last chapter. Margaret Beech states that "the only strong disadvantage that springs to mind is the lack of knowledge about medical or dental history that may exist in my [biological] family." On the more psychological side, Tony Pine writes: "It's much harder to discover your own character. You can't trace your personality or talents through your family. They have no guide as to what you're going to turn out like, and they encourage you to be like them and respond and develop like them."

From these quotations, it would appear that some adoptees are very conscious of the lack of a physiological link with their adoptive parents, and that this may affect them in one of two ways. Some feel it mainly as a *practical* drawback – that genetic knowledge might be useful to them, medically or psychologically. For others, the lack is more of an *emotional* one. One or two whose experience of adoption was not happy, attribute their feeling of "an absence of belonging" directly to the lack of blood relationship. It may be recalled, however, that George Sycamore – whose adoption was highly successful – expressed the view that not being a blood relation positively helped with any friction between himself and his adoptive relatives. These findings suggest to me that it is not the case that blood is necessarily thicker than water, but that this assumption may be invoked (despite the frequent cases of children abused or neglected by their biological parents) by those adoptees whose experience of adoption has been unsatisfactory.

Associated though not identical with the question of blood-relationship, is what might be termed the "reproval syndrome". A few of my contributors commented that when they were admonished in childhood by their parents, they often became very conscious of their adoptive status. Sylvia Rowan, for instance, writes: "I remember whenever I was told off for being naughty, I would always tell my adoptive mother that I wanted to run away to my biological mother." And Mrs Kate Poplar writes: "When I was tiny and my mother used to tell me off, I always crept away to my room and thought 'I bet my real mother wouldn't do that', although on adult reflection I have no doubt she would."

The issue here is not the fact of being reprimanded – which, as Mrs Poplar implies, inevitably happens from time to time during childhood. It is the fact that certain adoptees, under the stress of being scolded – or perhaps punished – and experiencing the natural resentment that most of us feel in such circumstances, may put the blame on the adoption. Or, possibly, they find that the recollection at that point of being adopted makes the reprimand actually easier to take – in which event this phenomenon should not, strictly speaking, be regarded as a drawback.

One serious factor, however, which certainly earns a place in this chapter, is the tendency which at least one adoptive parent had – as I learned with horrified surprise – to throw the fact of adoption in the face of the child, when annoyed with him/her. Thus part of a letter from Mrs Rosemary Larch (early thirties, adopted at fourteen months and brought up as an only child) reads: "I vividly remember having an argument with my mother, before I was at school, and she threatened to send me back to the Adoption Society. I never really felt close to her after that, I lost my trust of her."

14

Two other very serious allegations were made by Mrs Sheila Pear (adopted at two and a half years and now in her late forties, brought up as an only child). The relevant paragraph of her letter reads as follows: "All ties with my old life were severed, clothes and toys were burnt or given away. I remember a brown plush rabbit going and my distress . . ." and also, "I was told about the adoption badly, aged seven and a half – insecure from then on . . . My mother told me I was 'very difficult' between the ages of seven and eleven – I wonder why?"

These extracts from Mrs Pear's letter are enlightening as well as disturbing. They illustrate three points – all of which are discussed later (Chapter VII): first, the age at which to adopt, if given a choice; second, how to treat toys, clothes, etc., of which the adoptee may be fond; thirdly, the age at which the child should be informed of his adoptive status.

Mrs Jane Hawthorn, now in her early forties, was adopted at six weeks and, seven years later, her parents adopted a baby boy of three months. Mrs Hawthorn is happily married and has three teenage children. Although her adoptive mother was "a very maternal woman . . . who lavished much love and attention" on her, she did encounter a number of problems during her childhood, as a result of her adoptive status. "Although my maternal grandfather was very thrilled about having me, my paternal grandparents did not consider me as their grandchild. This attitude was to become quite prevalent in my early life from children of my parents' 'friends'. 'You don't belong to your mother', was a remark I had from some fellow-pupil at school. Some well-established friendships of my parents ended because of the friends' attitude towards me as being someone not to be quite sure about. Therefore I built a barrier around myself and when we moved after the war to Hull I told no one about the adoption . . . There is always lurking in the background the thought: 'Is my [biological] mother still alive? . . . Why did she let me go for adoption?' I have never got over the feeling of rejection by outsiders and the curiosity of them so I still do not tell anyone about it. In fact my husband told the two older children."

Edward Coppice, one of the two correspondents who elected to write anonymously, could find only one disadvantage, namely "the fact that adoption may lead to spoiling a child". This hazard does, of course, exist also for children born to their parents. Indeed, the remainder of this chapter is concerned with drawbacks described by contributors – which they saw as a result of their having been adopted but which I believe can, and sometimes do, apply equally strongly in the case of biological families.

The most frequently mentioned of these was being an only child. Most adoptees who were brought up without siblings – either adoptive or biological – express regret on this point. Tony Pine, for instance, writes: "There are various aspects of my character and development which I have at times ascribed to my adoption, but which are really due to the fact of being an only child. Since I am both an only and an adopted son it has not always been easy to separate the two." He goes on to say how much he appreciated living near to his cousins, and that "because they liked me so much, whenever I went to tea they would fight each other bitterly over who was to sit next to me."

Mrs Ruth Willow, however, whose parents were in their late forties when they adopted her – and who brought her up as an only child – describes her childhood as "lonely, as their [her parents'] friends' children were all older than I and my youngest cousin was six years older." Moreover, she felt that there was "no deep maternal affection" at home. Similarly, Mrs Kate Poplar's parents were in their forties when they adopted her and she "was brought up as an only child as they were considered too old to adopt another child". She has several children born to her (number not stated in her letter) and she believes that they have a much closer relationship with her than she had with her mother: "They are beautiful kids who certainly talk to me a lot."

Mrs Edith Maple was also brought up as an only child but she was treated with "Victorian" strictness – to use her own phrase (see pages 29–31 for her full letter). She suggests that the exceptional austerity with which she was reared was due to her parents' fear of "what would come out" in her perhaps because her biological mother was unmarried.

I gain the impression from Mrs Maple's letter that her adoptive parents would very likely have brought up a child born to them in accordance with the same stringent principles. But she is probably right in her supposition that her parents "were afraid what would come out" in her – because her biological mother had been unmarried. One or two people expressed a similar attitude to me when I told them that I was seeking two infants for adoption. They gave strong advice (unsought) against the project, actually declaring that "bad stock will out, you know", presumably having in mind the

16

illegitimacy of most children who are available for adoption and, evidently, unaware of the large number of children born to unwed parents, some of whom later get married, at least for a time.

Another possible snag mentioned by several of my correspondents was their failure to get on well with a brother or sister – the other side of the only child coin. Such failure seems to occur equally frequently between adopted siblings as between one adopted and one biological (or, perhaps I should add, between two biological siblings). It is well known that after a childless couple have adopted a child, the wife then sometimes conceives and bears a child – having waited frustratedly for this for many years. Thus some of the siblings in my sample were adopted-biological and others were adopted-adopted.

Clashes even between biological siblings, in childhood and in adulthood, occur quite often, and one hears the explanation "we are so much alike" about as frequently as one hears the opposite, "we're so very different". Precisely the same two opposing reasons are often given in explanation of the fact that two people get on exceptionally *well* together! Reading and re-reading my letters from adoptees and from adoptive parents, I formed the impression that warm, lasting affection occurs between adopted siblings just about as often as it does in biological families.

Let us end this chapter with a thoughtful, frank and moving statement from Sylvia Rowan. She writes: "I have been pregnant myself by someone whom I loved and do feel that in some way pregnancy and childbirth are a crucial part of the parent/child bond. The adoptive parents are ignorant of this part of the adopted child's life so I do not feel the bond can be absolutely complete in regard to this fact. I also feel that when the child is wanted, a new-born baby is the product of a love and is like a combination of the two people who created it . . . I wish in some ways that I was the genuine offspring of my adoptive parents and used to fear that I might, like my adoptive mother, be unable to conceive. I do believe that adoption is a good thing but I cannot say that I think it can quite match the couple who bears its own children. Incidentally I am unmarried."

III

Selected Narratives from Adoptees

Chapters I and II may strike the reader as over-analytical in approach. It may well appear arbitrary to isolate certain comments from the accounts of adoptees, to present them out of context, and to designate these comments as expressions of "advantages" and "drawbacks" – even in view of the fact that my circular letter was couched in those terms. As stated earlier, I chose that wording because I wished my request to be open-ended: to encourage those who did respond, to do so in as free-ranging a way as possible. I therefore avoided the use of a conventional questionnaire with its inevitably leading questions. But I had learned long ago that a *completely* open-ended invitation, such as "write an essay on any topic you like" or "tell me about your personal experience of adoption" has a curiously inhibiting effect on many people.

As will be seen in this chapter, some contributors did take me literally and tried to reply in terms of specific pros and cons. Others virtually free-associated to the concept of Adoption. Whilst yet others sent me a brief – in some cases, a not-so-brief – autobiography. I found that all were interesting and all were relevant to my aims, namely, to discover how well adoption "works" for both generations and to gain some guidance on how its workings may be improved.

Chapters I and II, however, may produce a somewhat disjointed impression, and they scarcely enable the reader to form a clear image of the individual adoptee. For these reasons, in the present chapter I employ a more holistic approach. I have selected twelve contributions, each being given *in toto*: the only changes, as before, are of place-names and people's names. The accounts are representative in that they span the whole spectrum from joyful acceptance to angry rejection and that age-at-adoption ranges from a few days to several years.

The selection is *un*representative, however, in one respect: for obvious reasons I have excluded very long accounts – some covering as much as eight or ten pages. This has perhaps resulted in the exclusion of those contributors who tended to ramble diffusely. On the whole theirs were among the less happy histories. Adoptees, like reviewers of books and plays, are liable to have more to say when making adverse criticism than when expressing satisfaction. Perhaps this is a universal phenomenon.

Let us begin with the response elicited from Michael Elm. In reply to my circular letter, he wrote as follows:

Dear Doctor Heim,

A copy of your letter dated the 25th September last has recently come into my hands, with the suggestion that I might be able to help you with your project.

I was adopted at the age of four and a half years of age, for whatever reason I have never known and now at the age of fifty-two, I look back on the years with my adoptive parents with a mixture of sadness and surprise that I was eventually able to escape by leaving home and having to learn to live.

How long after my own adoption I cannot remember, but I believe about two years, a girl of two years or thereabouts was adopted. If anything her fate was even worse than mine! There are now, thankfully, various agencies who can and do, in the main at least, prevent such happenings. My adoptive parents had no biological children.

You will by now have gathered, I can see no advantages in adoption, rather the reverse. However, the drawbacks we encountered were many, the chief of which I suppose being the lack of natural parents. We felt, and I think were regarded as, somewhat out of the ordinary, and had I not left when I did, I think the damage would have had a permanent effect.

Ours was a particularly unfortunate experience. I am sure your research reveals a much happier experience taken overall. I should be grateful of your findings. There are whole areas of my life which may have been different, given a happier beginning. However, I have a very happy marriage, with two teenage children, one at

19

Warwick studying Philosophy, and one about to take Arts A-levels. Their mother is a hospital almoner. Naturally, I'm very proud of them all. So you see, I have been more than compensated.

There is after all a compensation! A purely personal one I admit. I had to fight to survive, and I was given some wonderful friends and a very understanding wife, without whom I might not have survived, and a large measure of stamina.

If I can be of further help please do let me know.

Yours sincerely,
Michael Elm

I found this letter intensely interesting – but also baffling, since however many times I re-read it I was unable to discover what it was that had constituted such a "particularly unfortunate experience" for Mr Elm and his adopted sister. I therefore sent him the following letter:

Dear Mr Elm,

Thank you so much for your letter of 10th December. I am very grateful to you for co-operating in my research – and especially for your kind offer of further help. If I may take you at your word, you could indeed be of further assistance, in two ways.

First, it would be exceedingly helpful if you could give me, say, three or four specific examples of the drawbacks of adoption, as experienced by you. I get only the general picture from your letter, and this is not quite enough for my purpose. I realise that I may be asking you to do something rather "tough": that my request may involve you in reliving painful experiences – and I am very sorry. But if you can bring yourself to spell out the problems, it may well prove helpful to me in the writing of my book and, hence, to future adopters and adoptees.

Secondly, would you be kind enough to pass on the enclosed circular letter to your adopted sister? Or, if you prefer, let me have her name and address and I will send her the letter direct.

I am really very grateful.

Yours sincerely,
Alice Heim

In reply, I received the following answer:

Dear Dr Heim,

Thank you for your letter of the 18th December: please accept my apologies for the delay in answering.

I should I think [*sic*] say immediately that whilst I would be prepared to provide further background, the problems I encountered were a result of the mental make-up of my parents, and would probably have occurred anyway. They were not due necessarily to the adoptive relationship.

However, two problem areas existed for me, which may be as relevant today as they were then: (a) For me, the absence of a blood relationship proved a problem, in that I felt an absence of belonging. Very careful and prolonged counselling may well have overcome this.

(b) Perhaps more important to the adoptee is the need for supervision of the adoption, either by the Court at which the adoption Order was made, or through the Local Authority. I have no doubt that, in the case of my sister and myself, such supervision would have prevented much hardship.

My sister unfortunately died some while ago in Australia, and I have to return the copy of your letter.

Thank you for your good wishes. I wish you and the future book every success. Naturally, if you feel I can be of any further help please do not hesitate to write again.

Yours sincerely,
Michael Elm

This time I did not take advantage of Mr Elm's offer to be of further help as I thought it unlikely that I would gain enlightenment by so doing. Despite an element of self-contradiction in his second letter, it seems clear that, for him, adoption is felt to be intrinsically unsatisfactory ("absence of a blood relationship"), but that he felt also that his parents were unsuited to parenthood – whether adoptive or biological. It is perhaps noteworthy that both Michael and his sister were several years of age at the time of adoption.

Let us turn now to the correspondence I had with Mrs Audrey Medlar. In response to my circular letter she wrote as follows:

Letter I

Dear Dr Heim,

My father, Dr Yew, passed on your letter to me. I am willing to co-operate, but I thought that your letter was rather vague. However, I am not really sure what it is that you want to know. You mentioned "the advantages and the drawbacks that you have encountered, as a result of being adopted". It is, of course, difficult to recognise any of these things as direct results of being adopted or as mere problems and joys of childhood. If you could be more specific I would be grateful.

I am eighteen years old and was brought up with my adopted brother who is two years younger than me. I was six weeks old when my parents first had me and three months when everything was finally legalised.

I would be happy to help you further, and wish you every success with your book.

Yours faithfully
Audrey Medlar

I replied, explaining why my letter was "rather vague" and – without mentioning any specific points – expressing the hope that she would indeed help me further. In reply, I received the following letter:

Letter II

Dear Dr Heim,

I am sorry that I have been so late in producing this somewhat short essay. I hope it is still useful to you. If I can be of more help please let me know.

I was adopted at the age of six weeks so my parents are the only ones I have known. For as long as I can remember, I have known that I was adopted. To me adoption was something special – my parents had chosen me – it was not until I was much older that I understood about my natural mother getting pregnant without being married and thus being unable to keep me. Therefore, I have never felt unwanted.

I have always felt that my parents have concentrated on bringing myself and my brother up in the best way possible. I was

22

sent to a grammer school for girls where I got a good number of O-levels and three A-levels. I rejected university and later any form of further education, which may have upset my father who is an Oxford Graduate, and decided to marry on leaving school; but surely these feelings are apparent in many parents. Here, I feel that my parents may have been more upset than natural parents, perhaps they felt I was saying, "Well, you've brought me up for eighteen years – thanks, I'm off now." They needed reassuring that this was not the case.

My parents, I feel, have always emphasised that I am no different to anyone else – almost to the point of "brainwashing", but I have now been able to think about the situation myself and decide for myself, and I agree with them.

I have never felt any desire to find my natural mother as I am aware of the upset it could bring her, my parents and possibly myself.

I sometimes consider the possibility of being adopted by someone else – or being aborted – but these did not happen so I do not dwell on them – although we joke that my brother would have been happier in a rich man's family!

On the whole, although people say the most ridiculous things and look on me as somewhat different, I am just the same as anyone else, as is my relationship with my parents.

Yours,
Audrey Medlar.

I gain the impression from Audrey Medlar's two letters that she has had a happy, fulfilled childhood and adolescence, and that she has had some success in avoiding being "brainwashed". Her concern for the feelings of her adoptive parents – and also for those of her biological mother – is a recurring theme in many of the letters I have received. It is clearly apparent in the following letter, from Mrs Jane Hawthorn:

Dear Dr Heim,
I have received a copy of your letter from a friend who knows that I was an adopted child.
I was adopted at the age of six weeks in 1938. My adoptive mother had undergone a hysterectomy at the age of twenty-nine which ended any chance of her having her own family. She is a

very maternal woman and it must have been a bitter blow. However she was fortunate to have a very helpful family doctor who helped her enormously to be able to adopt me.

Of course at the age of eighteen months the 2nd World War broke out and my father went into the Air Force leaving my mother and I in a West Midlands town. My father was a Bank clerk. Therefore much love and attention was lavished on me by my mother. However although my maternal grandfather was very thrilled about having me, my paternal grandparents did not consider me as their grandchild. This attitude was to become quite prevalent in my early life from children of my parents' "friends". "You don't belong to your mother" was a remark I had from some fellow-pupil at school. Some well established friendships of my parents ended because of the friends' attitude towards me as being someone not to be quite sure about. Therefore I built a barrier around myself and when we moved after the war to Hull, I told no one about the adoption. I grew up quite like my mother in build, colouring and looks except that she has brown eyes and I have blue.

In 1945 my parents adopted another child – a boy of three months, one of the many unplanned war babies. I always seemed to know more about his background than about my own of which I know nothing and I never like to ask for fear of hurting my parents, who would feel that they had not done enough for me or been proper parents.

I was able to stay at school until I was eighteen and then go on to Reading University to take a post graduate certificate in Education. I then taught in a girls' Grammar school until I married a Solicitor whom I had met in Reading.

I have three children of my own aged eighteen, sixteen and ten and when I look at them I wonder about my natural parents and how much of their looks and character may come from their maternal natural grandparents. Of course when I was pregnant my mother could not give me any first-hand experience, which may have been a good thing!

I was told about the adoption from my earliest years. "You were chosen" was the expression used.

There is always lurking in the background the thought: Is my mother still alive? Are there any half brothers and sisters? Why did she let me go for adoption? What is my background?

Medically, of course, I do not know whether my parents are alive or what illnesses are a family trait.

I have never got over the feeling of rejection by outsiders and the curiosity of them so I still do not tell anyone about it. In fact my husband told the two older children.

I realise that these days the attitudes are different but still friends, who do not know I am adopted discuss the subject and say they could never do it themselves, and two sets have gone childless rather than adopt so the prejudices are still there in some cases.

Moreover the adopted child may have many fantasies as to who their parents are, which is not open to natural children. However, accompanying the thoughts are ones of guilt because of the gratitude and debt owed to the parents who brought one up and the fear of hurting their feelings if one makes too many enquiries. When the new law came in a few years ago about tracing one's parents I felt a great curiosity and desire to try but my husband reasoned me out of it and I couldn't bear to hurt my parents who are getting on now and to whom I owe a great deal.

I do hope that this ramble will be of help to you in your survey and if I can be of further help to you I would be most willing. As I expect you can tell I am rather sensitive about the subject but am considered quite well adjusted and sensible amongst those who know me.

Best wishes for your book

> Yours sincerely,
> Jane Hawthorn

P.S. I am sorry that this is at the last minute but I am a rather busy lady with family and charity work – my debt to society?

Although Mrs Hawthorn pays tribute to the loving care she has received from her parents, she evidently suffered quite severely – and understandably – from feelings of rejection, largely inspired by the negative attitude of her paternal grandparents and of various friends of her parents. She is, of course, mistaken in her belief that fantasies about their parents are "not open to natural children".

Such fantasies are not only open to them but are frequently entertained – sometimes pleasurably, sometimes distressingly.

The next letter is from Richard Plane. Although he writes articulately and vividly, his original spelling suggests that this may have been a major problem for him: indeed, his handwritten letter gives the impression of some degree of dyslexia.

Dear Dr Heim,

I received your letter with interest and I shall be glad to co-operate, with as much information as possible.

Sex: male
Present Age: 23
Date of Birth: 1956 [given in full]
Date of Adoption: 1956 [given in full]
One sister age 21, adopted

I work in the Haematology Department of X Hospital [name given], as a medical laboratory technician. I have worked four years in laboratories and am doing day-release HNC.

I think the main advantage of being an adopted child is knowing that I was wanted by a loving parent. This is possibly something most children never even question.

When I was told I was adopted at a very young age I received the news with somewhat indifference, mainly because I had no other pre-adoption experience to compare [sic].

Another advantage which has probably a greater influence on my development is that my adopted parents are possibly better suited to bringing up children from the moral, intellectual, social and financial aspect than my natural mother. If my natural mother felt that she had to give me away because she was unable to care for me, either mentally, physically or financially, then I have obviously been better off with my adopted parents. This is though hypothetical as I don't know the situation that faced my natural mother all those years ago. The possibility that I am the illegitimate son of a famous family cannot be ruled out; which brings me to the drawbacks of adoption.

Since the fairly recent Act, enabling adopted people to trace their natural mothers back, with the help of previously very confidential files, I have no desire to trace my origin or family (natural) history.

Natural questions from close friends who find out that I was

26

adopted (I don't keep it a dark secret) always wonder why I don't want to know who my mother was, but the only mother I have known is the one that adopted me, and therefore to me, my natural mother.

Perhaps the questioner infers my lack of identity should be corrected [sic]. As both my sister and I were adopted we have completely different characters which produced tensions during our teens. Whether this animosity was because of our normal growing up rebelliousness or a result of coming from different parents and hence no innate closeness remains an unanswered question. I suspect that our different origins had very little to do with these tensions, and was just a personality clash.

Until you wrote to me I had forgotten I was adopted, it's not the sort of subject I constantly think about therefore I think adoption has not affected me at all psychologically, and must have benefited me greatly.

If you require any further information I shall be glad to oblige.

Yours sincerely,
Richard Plane

One of the interesting points in Richard's letter refers to the tensions and animosity subsisting between him and his adopted sister. My own observations suggest that discord between biological siblings during and after childhood is not at all uncommon.

The next letter is atypical of those quoted in that I know the writer, personally. Mrs Mary Fir is a friend of longstanding friends of mine. I had met her three or four times, unaware that she was adopted. Then, in the course of discussing this projected book, she told me that she was adopted and she immediately offered to contribute. Since several of the other adoptees are personally known to me, I thought that the inclusion in this chapter of one such narrative would improve the balance:

Dear Alice,

Thanks for the circular letter about your book. I am fifty, was adopted at about ten days, I think, and it was illegal, just handed over (like a parcel I suppose!) As you know, I'm married and have two daughters.

My mother who brought me up had no money and no education, but always followed her strong impulses. How she

27

managed to convince her husband and parents I'll never know, they thought her somewhat irresponsible yet went along with it all.

Of my true parents I know nothing, partly because I don't think Mum and Dad knew much themselves, quite genuinely, but mostly because I knew they would be hurt by my wanting to know.

The psychological factors we nowadays take into account meant nothing to them, and led to some strange paradoxes.

My upbringing was punctuated by frequent comments: "Where would you have been if I hadn't taken you in, when your own mother didn't want you?" At an early age I needed to become mature enough to dissemble, and smile gratefully while squirming inwardly, because I didn't want to hurt them at all.

Yet it was not acceptable for me to ask bluntly just where I would have been, and why: I had to recognise their vulnerability whilst hiding mine. But it did me no harm.

Though I like the honest relationship I have with my children, there are odd times when I wonder if a little more sensitivity, even though contrived, might not be a bad thing! This possibly has less to do with adoption than with society in general, as we now live in a more articulate, and outwardly less respectful, age, don't you agree?

We got on very well. I loved and respected them both very much, and they gave me excellent opportunities educationally which they could really ill afford, and for which I am always most genuinely grateful.

A sad effect of the ignorance of basic psychology at the time, was that my sister has always been badly jealous. Easy to see, in retrospect, how a five-year-old would suffer at the intrusion of a mere baby for whom she was totally unprepared, especially as I suppose she would have just started school. She was also told by a mischief-making adult that "her nose would be out of joint now, but it was wrong because she was their own little girl". People say terribly irresponsible things, and I regret to say Judith's life was soured by jealousy. Ironically I got on much better with our parents than she did, which didn't help matters.

Generally speaking I think that advantages of having been adopted are (a) obviously a family home offers something no orphanage could ever provide. (b) Knowing no genetic background possibly makes one have an inner self-reliance, you are what you are as an individual, not slotted into a family tree of already established traits. (c) As a natural mother myself, I now realise how strong a bond exists between parent and child, and admire even more people who adopt and forge this bond themselves, without help from nature.

Disadvantages are very minor. (a) One doesn't have any health record, though probably nowadays one does actually, for any hereditary weaknesses. (b) Curiosity is very strong, to know what your natural place in a family tree would be, but again, nowadays this is encouraged I believe. (c) The feeling that one has to constantly prove one's affection, and worthiness, but is this confined solely to adoptees, probably not?

Do hope it is of some small help, and that you can read it. Look forward to reading your book.

Best wishes,
Mary

Despite the fact that Mary Fir and I know each other socially, there appears to be no essential difference between her letter and the other replies that I have quoted – and this is true, I think, of the other accounts from friends and acquaintances of mine.

Where Mary writes regretfully of the contemporary decrease in "sensitivity, even though contrived", I think that I should probably use the word "tact". Today's young people strike me as quite sensitive with respect to their own feelings but occasionally impatient of the need for tact where their elders are concerned. It seems to be likely that this is what Mary Fir has in mind.

The next letter is included as it is one of the few that tells of a failed first marriage, and of the behind-the-scenes manner in which the adoptee learned something of her biological background:

Dear Dr Heim,

I have had your letter passed to me by a friend Janice Lichen as she knows that I am adopted. I am female, aged forty-four years, and was adopted at the age of eighteen months.

My parents when they adopted me were aged approx. thirty-seven and thirty-nine years. I was told as soon as I was old enough to understand that I was adopted and that my parents chose me. I imagined that we were all lined up and I was the one they picked!!

I was always told never to tell anyone that I was adopted, but I did tell my friends at school and have never concealed it as I got older.

You ask one to write the advantages and drawbacks. I can think of no advantages – although perhaps if I had not been adopted I would have been brought up in a Home – which would have been a disadvantage.

I have never been told anything of my background but once when I was in my early teens I looked through my father's desk and found all the papers relating to my adoption, and found that my real mother was unmarried and learnt my real name – my parents do not know that I did this.

I think that my upbringing was unusually strict, partly I think because my parents were afraid what would come out in me – perhaps because my real mother was unmarried. My mother had been brought up herself in a very strict Victorian family and this reflected on her attitude towards me, e.g. no TV, radio, knitting, etc., on Sundays. Also I was never allowed to take friends or boyfriends home.

They have always been good to me in many ways – they gave me a good education and they still worry greatly about me, and my mother does not now think I am capable of bringing up my own children properly. But I think this a general attitude of parents.

When the new laws were passed regarding adoption I had no desire to contact my real parents, as I feel no good would come from this as they are not my parents, only through blood relationship. Perhaps if I was ever very lonely I may feel differently about this. I think occasionally, if one is depressed one thinks that one has no blood relations, and knows nothing of one's background or medical history.

It was *terribly important* to me to have children of my own as they would be my only known blood relations. I now have two lovely children.

My first marriage was not a success – partly I think because I married my first husband because of his parents. The first time I stayed with them, they took me into their hearts and I was like a daughter to them, and they gave me family love such as I had not experienced before. I was divorced and have remarried and am extremely happy with two children from my second marriage, but I still stay with my first husband's parents and my children are like grandchildren to them – it sounds terribly complicated, but it isn't!!

I do not think about being adopted, but I don't really think perhaps that I love my parents quite in the same was as I would if they were my own – but then I have never known anything else so I can't be sure.

They do not come to our home often – perhaps once a year and we only live a few miles from each other, and I always have to visit them by prior appointment – I cannot drop in, which I think is rather unusual and rather sad.

I am sure there are lots more things I could say but I can't think. If you do want to ask me anything, please do write to me or ring me, and I shall be only too glad to help in any way I can. Only good can come from your book I am sure.

Oh, I forgot I was the only child. My mother did have a miscarriage after she adopted me, which I think I was always rather relieved about! Then I shall never know!

I do hope to have been of some help to you.

Yours sincerely,
Edith Maple

This piece of autobiography gives rather a sad picture of adoption: a rigid and repressive upbringing followed by an unsuccessful first marriage (and, incidentally, an obliquely pathetic monochrome of the first husband). The second marriage sounds very satisfactory but evidently, Mrs Maple's relations with her adoptive parents remain formal and distant.

The next narrative, by Geoff Ebony, is included because Mr Ebony is himself a writer and it would seem a pity to exclude such a contribution from a book of this kind. His account contains rather more philosophising and less hard fact than many of the others, but much of the theorising is interesting – especially on the topics of parent/child resemblance, his idea of a "clean genetic sheet", and the sense of obligation felt by an adoptee. I shall refer back to these in a later chapter.

From Geoff Ebony

I cannot remember a time when I was not aware that I was an adopted child. I knew that I was "adopted" long before I understood anything at all about how babies are conceived or born.

My first clear memory of discussing adoption with my mother is associated with a car, a country lane with overhanging trees, and a hot summer's day. I assume we were driving down to see my grandmother in Dorset, I might have been six or seven, my younger sister (non-adopted) was with us and we talked as one does talk on long car journeys (there is no more intimate a situation, after all).

I don't remember that this discussion had any effect on me whatsoever, but I suppose the very fact that I remember the incident at all is significant.

If there were awards for adopting parents mine would unquestionably cop a Nobel Prize. They never made any secret of the fact that I and my elder sister were adopted, and that my younger sister was not, and though I suppose the *quality* of their love for us differed as between the adopted and non-adopted (there is something in the belief that blood is thicker than water) the *quantity* never varied. They did not have to make an effort to love me as much as my younger sister because they simply did. I felt no difference because there really was no difference. My experience is that most parents love their children in subtly different ways by virtue of the elementary fact that all their children are individuals.

A loving home-life enabled me to withstand the rigours of a ghastly prep school, run on mid-Victorian lines, and guaranteed me a happy childhood. My adolescence was full of the usual turmoils and is of little interest to anyone except possibly me. The pains and pressures I endured had nothing to do with the fact that I was adopted. I never thought about the matter. If it ever came up in discussion I was able to talk about it in a detached way (if any adolescent is ever detached).

As I grew more interested in other people and less absorbed with myself, in other words when I began to grow up, I noticed a curious phenomenon.

My father was an extremely eminent surgeon with a vast practice. It seemed that one could hardly go to any social gathering without meeting one or more of his patients. Many times I have been approached by beaming strangers who have said: "You must be Harold Ebony's son." They might add some standard waffle about spitting images and chips off old blocks. It was puzzling. How could an adopted child resemble his father? Coincidence? There are general physical types, after all. In my case this could not possibly be. My father was tall, lean, handsome and very distinguished-looking. I was short, baby-faced, stocky – from a totally different mould.

The theory I have formulated, to explain the fact that people quite genuinely saw a likeness between myself and my father where no likeness could possibly exist, is this: that mannerisms of speech and movement, even modes of thinking, are just as powerful recognition-signals as physical resemblance. Obviously I had absorbed a great many of my father's behavioural characteristics. I had *become like him*. In more than a legal or an emotional sense I was his son. Whatever I have inherited, genetically, from my real parents, has been so modified by the influence of my adopted parents that I could almost claim to be their child in terms of what I am.

To cast any real light on the situation I must compare my experience with that of my two sisters.

My elder sister has never been as stable or as secure as me. I think she has always felt out of place. She has always sought for relationships among the rich and the aristocratic, becoming a dedicated deb and an assiduous socialiser. I think she always felt cheated, because her own family was not as rich or as grand as she would have liked; and I am sure this had something to do with the fact that she was adopted. Perhaps she felt that she had been born to the purple and was having, through no fault of her own, to put up with tweed.

I never had any of these feelings. I have always identified (at some stages of my life fiercely) with the class into which I was adopted and which I suppose one would define as Professional Upper Middle. This seems to me to be the most fortunate stratum of our hyperstratified society, mainly because, in the long run, membership is based on merit rather than birth.

I am probably abnormal but I have always been slightly deaf to ancestral voices. Could this be because I am adopted? When I was feverishly being a poet (in my teens) I found it of very little interest indeed that my father was descended from a brother of Humphrey Ebony [an eminent writer]. My mother's family – all doctors, lawyers, clerics and actors on one side, shipowners and doctors (again) on the other – seemed to me to be a standard lot, who emerged from obscurity at the turn of the eighteenth century. Worthy but dull.

Later, at another stage of life, I came to think that it was a positive privilege to be adopted. One had started life with a clean genetic

33

sheet – origins unknown. One could make of oneself what one would. There were no hereditary factors to take into account.

This is a digression. I must return to the comparison with my sisters. My elder sister was always difficult and she has never, in spite of marriage and children, really cut the cord that binds her to her mother. Perhaps this is partly due to the fact that she was the first child, but I have always suspected that it was mainly due to the fact of her adoption. My younger sister cut herself off from her parents quite ruthlessly when she was nineteen/twenty and, having made her bid for freedom, established a completely mature and loving relationship with them. In this she was behaving like any normal, naturally born child.

My behaviour was quite different. I did cut myself off, as all children must if they are to become adults, but very gently, tactfully and slowly. My younger sister was completely open about her life, I was somewhat secretive. I divided my life into compartments. I let my parents see of me only what I thought would please them. The areas of my life which might have disturbed, shocked, or pained them, were discreetly veiled.

I am sure all this was done out of a sense of obligation; and a sense of obligation is probably the unique province of the adopted child. My younger sister did not feel she owed them anything. I felt I owed them everything. In my elder sister's case the sense of obligation is reversed. Her fundamental feeling is perhaps that *they* have an obligation to her, having taken her on. She had a much stormier and more passionate relationship with them than I did.

Having for most of my life considered the question of adoption as more or less irrelevant as far as I was concerned, I now face the fact that it might be very important indeed. My wife and I want to have a child. She feels very strongly that I should explore my genetic inheritance. I don't feel the need myself but this may simply be a defence-mechanism – one that has operated all my life. The clean slate/origins unknown syndrome may be simply the result of moral cowardice. As time goes by I do become more and more interested in my real heredity, but I tell myself that while my mother is still alive I should not go into it. But is this really the case? Am I perhaps frightened of discovering unpalatable facts, or even a flesh-and-blood person whom I would have to think of as mother or father.

The novelist in me says: there could be a good story here. My instinct for self-preservation says: leave well alone.

34

I do not know what the outcome will be. Probably I will investigate. I ought to be able to take it. I really am quite a balanced creature, after all, as balanced as to be the despair of anyone wanting to write a book about adopted children. Unless, of course, the majority of adopted children are emotional messes, psychotics, introverts and madmen, in which case I am an aberration.

Geoff Ebony

We have now seen enough narratives of adoptees to be able to assert that many are well contented with their adoptive parents and status. Thus Geoff Ebony is certainly no "aberration" – although he does perhaps find exceptional delight in his adoptive parents and, largely thanks to them, has attained a good measure of self-fulfilment.

The next contribution, from Mrs Phyllis Crabtree, is very much at the other extreme. I met Phyllis at a dinner party when I had already embarked on writing this book. In the course of conversation she volunteered the information that she was adopted and that her experience had been most unsatisfactory. She talked eloquently, bitterly – and even humorously – about it and I begged her to write a contribution for me. Within a few weeks I received the following letter (excerpts given here) and narrative:

Dear Alice,
   Herewith the magnum opus which is, I hope, as useful as you hoped it might be . . . There is not, I'm afraid much humour after all, I've discovered that it's probably only when I'm likely to be shy, as at dinner parties, that I engage my mouth without my brain and end up humorous!
   One aspect of the social background thing which I forgot to include and is worth at least a reminiscence is my constant amazement at the torpid ignorance of my family, e.g. . . . Tests carried out on my mother in hospital to see why she could not become pregnant were obviously no good. Nobody questioned why and she never knew why she could not have children. Her ignorance of her own body was profound and also of others! At ten years old I was accused of "doing something wrong" because she had noticed a discharge on my underclothes, this was immediately before puberty.
   I hope the book progresses well, and that my sisters contact you, which would be interesting. It would be safe to assume that if you

35

are conducting a free vote on adoption, I am against it and support the abortion laws with all my heart. I have known many others who were adopted and I think they would say the same. I am prepared to admit that the law of averages says it will work out now and again, but not often enough to make it a risk worth taking.

N.B. Throughout – "my mother, Mummy", etc., refers to my adoptive mother. Biological relations are referred to as "real". Very Freudian!

Sincerely,
Phyllis Crabtree

The day I discovered that I was adopted my mother had gone to court to formally adopt my four-year-old half-sister. I went home with another child from school and was taken to the child's mother, who knew where my own mother was that day and said to me, "So Mummy has three adopted children now." "Oh no," I replied, "I'm not adopted, I belong." But the remark stayed with me and when we were all home, I asked Mummy what the woman had meant. I was totally unprepared for the rage which followed.

I was accused of snooping at keyholes in order to come by the information and threatened with dire punishment if I ever spoke of it. I don't think I had really minded the reality of adoption until that moment, but the knowledge and the rage joined with a vague suspicion I always seemed to have had and made the idea horrible in every way. It was obvious in one second that the woman who had told me fully realised what she was doing and that my mother had never intended I should know. The world never seemed the same again. I was six years old.

My mother had worked as a daily help at the home of an officer of an adoption society. When one day my real mother came in with me at a few weeks old, to quote my mother, she "fell in love with me". She already had one adopted daughter, had another who had died at four years old, and was a widow who lived with her mother. She had lost her husband earlier that year. She asked my real mother if she could adopt me herself and by and large that is precisely what happened. Her wanting me, and the fact that she was already working for the society, secured me. And for the rest of my life I was expected to be grateful. Grateful that one woman saw me and wanted me, as one might covet something in a shop window and grateful that another woman did not want me and had sought the earliest opportunity of ridding herself of me. This sense of rejection was always far stronger to me than that someone had chosen to have me, for I always saw that my mother's maternal feelings did not stretch far beyond a child's reaching any kind of independence. In working-class rural areas, children and babies were made much of until they could answer back, then active affection ceased, usually being given to the next baby.

Most people's memories of childhood seem to largely blot out the nasty times and conveniently remember sunshine and happy times. I can honestly say that I can remember no happy times as a child. I can remember anxiety from my very earliest days and later on depression and increasing rages and frustration. I was around nine years old when I became convinced that my heart would stop beating and I should die. I was constantly feeling my heart to see if it had stopped and was terrified to go to sleep in case I never awoke again. I dared tell no one because I sensed that I should neither be understood nor comforted.

The anxiety gave way to some kind of breakdown and I was sent to stay with my real grandparents for a time. I imagine the anxiety arose partly from an inherently anxious nature and partly from the fact that I was in a family where everyone was so old. My mother was over forty before she adopted me. My grandmother nearly seventy. Their friends and relations seemed to be always old and ailing and worrying conversations were always conducted in front of us children, with no thought for childish imaginative horrors.

My imagination got me into a lot of trouble as a child. The real world was, to my mind, very dreary, and it was patently obvious that it held a lot less for me than for other children I knew, both materially and emotionally. The world of my imagination was infinitely superior but, as with most small children, the edges of the two worlds became blurred. This to my mother was arrant lying. As she was to do so often, she applied to higher authority, in this case my head-teacher. To her it was merely a lively imagination, an expression of intelligence but to my mother it was still "sinful lying".

The referring to higher authority was an almost constant event of my childhood. To me it seemed a tacit admission that she had no idea what children were all about, once they gave up bottles and napkins. As a young teenager, the village policeman was

37

called to me after an argument, because as she explained to him "she couldn't do a thing with me". The vicar, the local woman magistrate for whom she worked, and later on the local authority welfare officers and social workers were all called upon to do what she could not do. I was amazed that she could admit publicly that she could not do what she had wanted to do, namely bring up children. It was like going out and buying a puppy and rejecting it when it grew into a mature dog and stopped being pretty and playful.

I can still hear, and always will now, the things said which hurt me so dreadfully as a child. When talking of relations my mother would say, "He's my cousin, or uncle, or something, but of course he's no relation to you," or, more commonly: "He's nothing to you." When I grew older I always referred to her husband as just that, never "Daddy". She many times referred to the fact that her children were born "out of wedlock" which I thought was a town. After one of the terrible rows which she and I had when I was still only eleven or twelve in which I had begged her to tell me about my parents, she screamed at me, "Your father was a Yank, and that's what you are, a dirty Yank"! I was probably younger than eleven as I had no idea what a Yank was. When I won a scholarship to the grammar school, although she was proud, she only said, "You needn't think I'm keeping you at school till you're eighteen." Her constant remark when visiting the school was that anyone over the age of fifteen looked as though they ought to be at work.

Time and again remarks were made both in our hearing and to us which it would horrify me to have my children hear. I still have an abiding fear of the dark, planted in me when I was small by being told when naughty that "things" would get me in the dark. "Mind they don't grab hold of you" was a source of much amusement to everyone else, as I lay screaming in the dark. "It's only temper," I was told.

Being constantly misunderstood is the fate of many children, I'm sure, whether natural or adopted. As soon as I realised I was adopted I was certain that it was only for adopted children that such states existed. I can remember being really very small, probably only three, four or five, and being tickled to be made to laugh. I was a rather serious baby and child, in photographs I look like a doll, and the hysteria which these tickling bouts gave way to resulted in tears and sickness. But I was always told that I had "no sense of humour" because I did not laugh when tickled. To me it was torture not humour, and that no one saw this was ignorance bordering on sadism.

The things at which people laugh were both where I first saw divergences of interest and where the widest gaps of interest lay. My earliest memories were of the sheer vulgarity of what passed for humorous activity in my family. I became what they called "snobbish" at an immensely early age, and I have no idea how or why. In rejecting what they stood for, my values became those of a more affluent and intellectual class. I constantly aped those from middle-class backgrounds whose life-style more closely resembled the one I felt I could be comfortable in and wanted. Speech style, eating habits, pastimes, hobbies, in all these things I wanted only to be as different as possible from the family I was forced to call mine. Naturally, this led to a good deal of resentment from my mother. When I went to grammar school and had even greater opportunities of "social mobility", "She thinks she's too good for us now" was a cry I heard constantly. Indeed I did.

Perhaps two things remain above all else in my mind from childhood. Neither is peculiar to an adopted child, but both are indicators of the crime people, well-meaning people, commit against children, when they allow them to be brought up in a background in no way resembling their own and try to pretend it is normal or natural. It is neither and few children would ever believe it was.

The first thing was my longing for a father or a father figure. I used to "borrow" other children's fathers as a child, because Daddy was such a lovely word. Untypically, my mother gave me a photograph of my real father but when she saw how much it meant to me, she destroyed it. He was an American serviceman stationed here in the last war, very young and very handsome and I loved his photograph for it was all I had of him. My mother was jealous, so she destroyed him and I never forgave her. It doesn't need another Freud to see why I could find no happiness in marriage until I married someone just about old enough to be my father.

The second thing was the almost psychotic cruelty my mother could exhibit, in view of the fact that she had chosen to adopt three children. In retrospect, the cruelty arose from fear that she would not be loved, or jealousy, or bitterness that she could have no children of her own. But the terrifying cruelty that can lock children in cupboards, or lock oneself in a room and laugh at the child outside saying, "Come out, Mummy, I love you, I will be good," is still beyond my comprehension. Quite apart from the physical cruelty, actual and threatened. Irons have a horrid fascination as I can still remember being cornered and threatened with "branding".

My mother never understood that in order to hold on to children you have to let them go. She unashamedly told us, as we all left home to get married at very young ages, "I thought you would be a comfort to me in my old age," as though we had been purchased like an insurance policy. To the end of her life she exerted this moral stranglehold, and though I recognised it for what it was, so desperate was I for love and approval I usually succumbed, for paradoxically I was my mother's favourite child, and I think my sisters fared worse at her hands, which meant they could resist the moral blackmail better.

Only as I grew older did I understand what my mother was all about; the efforts to purchase love that she had made. A complete absence of discipline other than tempers and cruelty for: "I thought you wouldn't love me if I disciplined you." As a child I used to pretend that I had routine jobs to do and a strict discipline to adhere to, for I equated discipline with love – if people cared about you, then they tried to make you better people. My mother thought you bought love with indulgence, and flew into rages every time she found you didn't. She hoped that the self-righteousness she experienced every time she was told, in our hearing, "I think you're doing such a wonderful job," would compensate for the fact that the cuckoos in her nest very obviously didn't love her, couldn't love her.

I don't think I ever loved her and I often wished, as a child, that I had been brought up in a Home, though I have since realised that I might have been no happier there. But no one would have pretended that it was my home, and it was just like everyone else's, for it patently would not have been. The whole thing was a cheat, to my mind. When I realised that my real, natural grandparents were fairly middle-class (I spent quite a lot of time with them as a child) and that I was of this background, though not in it, it only increased my sense of being cheated and rejected. Very early on, I realised that the race is not only to the swift, but to those who start half way round the track, namely *anything* above lower, working class. I struggled against my background in order to maintain a place there, and consequently fitted in nowhere.

The day my mother died I felt relief; the day we buried her I felt

40

anger, because, I suspect, I had no other emotion to call on. The regrets are because she did not live to see that I am, at last, making a success of life, in material and emotional terms, and because I believe she truly did love my children and she was the only person who could share in the emotions I have about them. In the end it was our love for them that kept us together, and not love for each other, deeply as we both wanted it.

Unfortunately, Phyllis Crabtree's sisters did *not* contact me. I should have been particularly interested to hear from them, as this might have helped to check certain facts – some of which are hard to credit – and it might also have given some idea of how intrinsically difficult Phyllis had been to bring up. As it stands, her account suggests that she was a child who needed imaginative, highly intelligent, preferably professional parents – and that her adoptive mother was prosaic, markedly below average intelligence, widowed and, as Phyllis puts it, lower working class. One can picture the bewilderment and dismay of this mother finding that she has a wild cygnet in her home instead of the pretty, amenable duckling she had expected.

But in any case, certain of Phyllis' comments are instructive and may have a significance well beyond her particular experience. First is her mother's furious denial that Phyllis was adopted (alarming because it implies something shameful about adoption and because it became clear to the daughter that her mother was lying to her). Secondly, comes the puzzling and harsh insistence that her relatives were "nothing to" her daughter. Thirdly, we have the heartless destruction of the photograph of Phyllis' biological father – reminiscent of the burning of Sheila Pear's brown plush rabbit (page 15). And fourthly, Phyllis' clearsighted observation that "in order to hold on to children you have to let them go". This, of course, is true for all families but few biological parents, I think, would blatantly and self-pityingly reproach their children for marrying and hence being unavailable as comforters in the parents' old age. The fifth point of especial interest for me is Phyllis' equating of discipline with love. "If people cared about you, then they tried to make you better people." No doubt her poor mother did try so to do – but her methods would have suited few, if any, children.

The two next narratives are by a pair of siblings, Sarah Teak, née Alder-Buckthorn, and her (also adopted) brother, Adrian Alder-Buckthorn. She was the younger adoptee; indeed she had another

41

adopted brother, intermediate in age between Adrian and herself, but he lives abroad and I have been unable to contact him. As is seen below, Mrs Teak has had multiple sclerosis for some years. She wrote as follows

I dictated this to my husband from almost illegible notes written in fits and starts over one day in more of a conversational than a literary style

BRIEF DIGEST

Born legitimate daughter of composer/musicologist and wife, 1927, London. Adopted at birth as previously agreed – by Dr John Alder-Buckthorn, FRS, DSc, etc., and his wife. School in Scotland and a (Quaker) school in the North of England [names of both schools given] Matric. 1944; Central School of Speech and Drama, London – Diploma there. Career mainly as teacher of children in Drama, English; some adult teaching, coaching and remedial in English, variously in literature and spoken English as a Foreign Language. Married meteorological observer 1950, he at thirty, I at twenty-three. Son 1953, daughter 1956. Husband, subject to stress depression after war captivity, retired to other work 1960 and finally retired 1974 at age fifty-four. I retired 1976 because of multiple sclerosis that had attacked 1973. Our children are both well-rounded characters, stable, well-liked and at work. We maintain a traditional style of close family ties with all the Teaks and all the Alder-Buckthorns.

Born at a private nursing home somewhere in London 1927. Adoption arranged before birth, provided (I think) the baby was a girl. Biological mother in poor health and there were financial difficulties – there were four elder children. My [biological] father was a musician, later to be a Professor of Harmony [name of college given]. Mother had been a nurse. Sickly infant, probably due to mother's ill-health during pregnancy. For this reason I was christened at the Home but have always preferred to suppress this fact!

My adoptive parents were Dr John Alder-Buckthorn and his wife Lucy. He was a scientist of some distinction and to him and his wife I shall now refer as father and mother. Both were in their mid-forties and staunch Quakers. My name was changed to Sarah Lucy A-B. They already had two adopted sons, ten and seven years older than me (non-biological brothers).

Their old family Nanny came out of retirement to care for me. By nine years old I was a tough and active little tomboy with two adoring and adored much older brothers. We are still on the best of terms. They teased and protected me as other brothers and as we got older we talked openly with each other about our adoption but *never* to our parents.

I was not told about my adoption until I was about ten years old and it was a great shock. I remember the occasion and am sure Mother never meant to tell me in the way she did. I kept my feelings bottled up, having been brought up to be stoical and non-complaining but, for the next few years, it used often to distress me. This exacerbated by a knowledge of being less clever at school than befitted the child of my brilliant father and a mother who was distinguished in the town for her philanthropy and social concern. He was then Principal of the Technical College where many of my teachers taught in the evening – and knew him well. They seemed to expect me to be equally brilliant and I was just average. Saved at thirteen years from this unhappiness at school by being sent to a Quaker boarding school in X [name given] where I was very happy and blossomed in every way.

I loved my Mother very much. She was great fun and companionable. For my Father I had awe and respect but quite failed to appreciate his intellect until I was grown up.

I was always very embarrassed when the subject of "where were you born?, etc. came up and remember two terrible occasions when birth certificates had to be produced for some reason. This feeling lasted I think until after I was married. Perhaps it is significant that when sorting out papers after Mother's death (1957, when I was thirty), I threw away everything relating to my adoption including my adoptive parents' letters to the Matron of the Nursing Home which they had never shown me.

As a student in London at the Central School of Speech and Drama I had an urge to get in touch with my biological family but was dissuaded by my boyfriend, who said it would only cause embarrassment and distress to them, to my adoptive parents and to myself. He was possibly right (I was then eighteen), though I have since wished I had made contact. However, that could still happen as recently I have made some enquiries, but no luck so far. The boyfriend's advice is interesting because when I told him I was adopted he was most upset. He had hoped to marry me and produce a genius like John Alder-Buckthorn! I never forgave him

43

for that. When I subsequently told Nevil Teak when he asked me to marry him he was quite unperturbed (about my adoption!).

Before I went to London, Father gave me a book about music written by my biological father and a verbatim transcript of the entry in *Who's Who in Music* referring to him. John Alder-Buckthorn was afraid I might meet my "real" father and [thought] I should know as much about him as possible.

Re-reading that book recently I can see quite a lot of the author's character in my own. There is also a portrait sketch showing a marked facial resemblance. I tell my son, who is very like me, that is probably what he will look like when he is older. It is fascinating to speculate about my own children, both now in their twenties, as to inherited characteristics from their maternal grandparents. I *would* like to know more about my biological mother!

At times I long to know more about my "real" family but will always be immensely grateful to John and Lucy Alder-Buckthorn for giving me a wonderful start and happy childhood. They were rather old to take on another child but my mother was very young in spirit. I knew more about my biological parents than is usual and this is intriguing but there has always been a certain psychological barrier to finding out more.

Sarah Lucy Teak

The Alder-Buckthorn parents were Rh-incompatible and they decided to adopt after several miscarriages and deaths. John Alder-Buckthorn, FRS, was a polymath: physicist, philosopher, statistician, meteorologist, psychologist. He was also an idealist and a noteworthy eccentric. I remember, decades ago, attending a lecture by him and – although I can no longer remember the subject-matter – I vividly recall the combination of obscurity, erudition and very genuine idealism which informed it. I found it both impressive and confusing, and it is most interesting that some of the same qualities obtain in the contribution of his adopted son, Adrian (who became a motor engineer).

The format below is precisely as set out by Adrian – apart from the fact that he gave his address and telephone number at the top and that his typing was exceptionally closely spaced:

From Adrian Clifford Alder-Buckthorn

1Q The number, age and spacing of Adoption.

1A Three, Male 2½yrs; Male 6 mths (?); Female 6 mths (?) –
    Spacing 1–2=3 mths, 1–3=7 yrs.
2Q Any others born, etc: Approx 6 rhesus negative [sic] stillborn
    (up to & after adoption).
2A The hope was obvious for high intelligence progeny. For
    approx 4 years another whole family of 3 boys + 1 girl were
    brought up as family on holiday from boarding school – they
    were overseas missionary children.
3Q Experience of life, etc. etc.
3A A long complicated psychological, physiological and genetic
    research on its own! At this stage only a brief resumé, or scan,
    is possible. It is important to note that this review originates at
    the age of 63, when values may carry a totally different
    emphasis from those that existed at, say, ages 10, 30, 40, etc.
    Categories: a) Childhood; b) Adolescence; c) Adulthood (+
    possibly d) aspects in later maturity.

a) At an age of initial and retentive awareness – 3 yrs ± – normal
    reading of bible stories caused an intense (internal) feeling of
    "Prodigal Son" and almost "Cain & Able" [sic] thoughts, but
    not relationship, to a new brother who had *suddenly* arrived to
    share the *birth*right. This was never manifested, but existed,
    and unexpectedly seems to have built a very close, lasting but
    undemonstrative tie based on family but not so much *of*
    family. Our adoptive mother was certainly loving but rarely
    was demonstrably so. There certainly did, and does, exist an
    absolute understanding between three total variants. I was
    said to have a violent and uncontrollable temper, even at an
    age which I should remember (many different reports), but
    this I do not remember, I do remember that my independent
    nature and outlook was misunderstood, but I have usually
    been known as a very kind and considerate person. My
    marriage (late and without children) has been one of sheer
    bliss for thirty-two years. To revert a moment, as an example
    the first words at the first meeting after both had survived
    dangerous war service (parents were pacifist) were "do you
    remember we were discussing what happened to the old
    canoe we lost before the war" and the answer was "we decided
    that we would need to build another, well shall we start?" As
    you see, emotion was never allowed above the surface!

b) This was reduced by boarding school to the period of holidays
    and both (actually all three) having experienced severe anti-

English bullying at previous Scottish schools (could have originated from history teaching) formed even closer ties. Although certain outlets, e.g. Scouts, provided better contacts, life was lonely as somewhere inhibitions did appear to exist, also physical differences (5'6" vs 6'2") guided feet in different recreational paths, my brother went in for long-distance cycle touring – I was lazy. Although these differences, on reflection, were just as much psychological as adoptive (in terms of the family unit). Around this time a major formative factor occurred which relates to adoption by those with higher (much) mental, and maybe physical, talents than the average. I worked in helping my father in physical and other scientific experiments, i.e. seismology, radar initial development *1933/34*, time marking cathode ray oscillograph, meteorology (aged 7), psychology (as guinea pig), instrument making, scientific photography, study and investigation of cosmic and gamma rays etc., etc. Few of these items had I any basic grounding in, but absolute faith was placed in the accuracy of my assistance in advanced work which was mostly far beyond me in comprehension. Whereas my own interests were all centred around automobile technology in one form or another.

The fact that three children all had different "built in" aptitudes made it possible to develop personal interests, and careers, on a solitary personal basis but still maintaining the physical family framework. With parents of enormous intelligence objectivity [sic] we were allowed to develop without pressure, even being offered help in lines totally abhorrent to their principles, but I think that we must have been under genetic scrutiny. Probably being the oldest, I developed on the mathematical and physics field, although the engineering interests must have been inherited, brother was a more rewarding result qualifying as master mariner, degree in sociology and now working in medical foundation research, my sister developed inherited music and drama.

It could be noticed that ties with relatives were not quite as close, or closely maintained, as normal; this just as much on our side as theirs, a basic "tribe" element appeared to be missing, we all found fault with the clan's high image of itself (it did have a fairly high level position).

END

46

Let us end this chapter with two of the happiest accounts of adoption that I have received – from the brothers Rosewood. (Their parents' point of view may be found in Chapter V.) The Rosewoods was one of the few families of which all members felt able to respond to my circular letters:

Dear Madam,

I write in reply to your circular letter of last September on the subject of adoption. I am in a similar position to your own children being in my early twenties and having been adopted at only a few weeks old. I have a brother who was also adopted at a similar age.

In many ways, it is very difficult to think of any advantages or disadvantages as I have not known any other kind of upbringing. I genuinely feel that my life has not been in any way different from that of a child brought up by its natural parents.

I cannot actually remember a day when I was told that I was adopted, or, for that matter, being shocked by the news. I have been aware of being an adopted child for as long as I can remember and it has honestly never caused me a moment's worry.

In some respects I feel that I may have been given even more love and attention than a child with natural parents because my adoptive parents were so enthusiastic about having their own child that they were prepared to give all their love to someone else's child: the net result being very definitely a benefit to the child.

It can only be an advantage for a child to be adopted by people who want it, rather than being brought up by natural parents who feel that the child is a burden.

As for disadvantages, I can think of none at all. I don't feel any desire whatsoever to seek out my natural parents and will not do so.

To sum up my feelings, I must confess that life as an adopted child has been so normal that I have never, until now, thought of it in terms of advantages and disadvantages.

I'm afraid that these reflections will probably not help your research but these are nonetheless my feelings.

                    Yours faithfully,
                    Martin Rosewood

Dear Dr Heim,

I am sorry that it has taken me so long to write to you and

complete the report from the whole family, but being away from the family it has been all too easy to avoid putting down my views on adoption. I hope that what I have to say will be of some use to you, though I hardly think it will make very thrilling reading for you.

First some basic information you asked for: I am just twenty-two years old (some two years younger than Martin) and male. You asked for views on "advantages" and "disadvantages" of being adopted. I'm afraid I've never really thought of myself in these terms especially as I've never had anything to contrast with.

The most obvious comment to make is that I have never felt anything particularly different about being adopted. My parents never hid my true origins from me at any stage, both Martin and I knew from an early stage that we had been "picked up" from a maternity hospital. This, however, did not make that great an impression on me; I even remember my mother saying to me that she had not been able to have a baby, but even this knowledge did not affect me, in any emotional sense, that is. Before my teens I have quite vivid memories of people saying how much I looked like my mother and Martin like my father, and the family joking about this afterwards. I was also told about other children who were adopted.

Certainly during my childhood (before teens) I feel that the whole issue was never hidden, yet at the same time it wasn't shouted out from the tree-tops. I never remember feeling guilty or insecure in any way during this stage as a result of being adopted. There was no reason to feel insecure at this time anyway, I certainly did not lack for love or any sense of belonging, and the whole issue of adoption was never regarded as being that important, since it played very little role in day to day situations. I presume that other children did not consider adoption as a possibility, if they knew what it was, and because I didn't consider it a piece of vital information to be shared it was never discussed.

In my teens little changed – the whole issue was not seen to be important, and the observations of outsiders on links in character-istics between parent-child continued to keep us amused. At secondary school the question never came up – but I think I only told two of my closest friends, and that was in the sixth form during chats on topics connected with it – abortion, family, etc.

During this period I *thought* far more about who I might have been, but the happiness of the family situation kept any thoughts of being "inferior" or "different" well away. At about seventeen I came to realise how lucky I was as a result of being adopted, and my thoughts on the subject became more parent-centred, that is trying to see what adoption must have meant to them rather than what it meant to me. From this my feelings of gratitude for the kind of upbringing I had enjoyed were intensified and I saw adoption to be a very positive action. The only time I ever talked about adoption to fellow-students was when the topic of abortion came up and in reply to a view that adoption (as an alternative) was unsatisfactory because the child would not enjoy the security of knowing who his/her "real" parents were. If it is of any interest, I do believe that adoption is the strongest case for those who want to reduce the number of abortions being carried out in Britain, especially for couples who want children but will not consider fostering or adopting a child over four or five years old.

I have never wanted to know who my "real" mother and father were, I know their professions and that they lived in Aberdeen, but as to their names, or the name she called me, I've been told but have forgotten. I've no desire to look for them, nor would I want to meet them if the opposite was the case. To me adoption was full of advantages – in terms of family life, parental support and educational opportunities. I know that had I not been adopted I would be a very different person, but since I'm very happy with what I am, and those around me, I don't bother to think about "if" questions like that. I certainly don't think I've suffered emotionally from the knowledge of my adoption, I'm sure it must have helped, though, to have had a brother in the same boat.

I really couldn't list a series of disadvantages – I've never felt inferior, in any form to other children or that my relationship with my parents was somehow not complete. At no stage in my life, either, have I wanted to reject my past, nor felt any sense of grievance with my parents for adoption to be used as a basis for this.

In all honesty, I don't feel anyone else's child because the need to be related physically to parents doesn't seem that important a factor to me. Whether this will change at all if I have children of my own is a good question but, at the moment, I do feel – very much a product of my parents' love for each other – in a sense that I am very much the product of their "giving" over the last twenty years. That I was conceived as the result of a relationship between

49

two others doesn't bother me; I'm grateful to the woman who gave birth to me – for having the courage not to abort and to give me for adoption – but beyond that my "parents" in every sense of the term are the two people who took over from there.

I do hope that some of this is of use, I'm sorry it's in no real logical order – I didn't feel I should try to think things out too logically because I've never really bothered to think too much about the difference adoption has made to me. As I said, I can't see any disadvantages for me in what has happened and I'll leave it to you to decide why this is so – though I'd be happy to point you in the direction of my parents for the answer.

If there is anything else you would like to know, if I've omitted anything as well, please don't hesitate to follow up this letter and, naturally, I shall be interested to read your conclusions to your study on adoption. I wish you every success in your work.

Yours sincerely,
Keith Rosewood

Both these letters give evidence of an exceedingly happy family situation – and the older generation confirms this in their letters, quoted on pages 78–82. It is interesting that Martin and Keith should have such different styles of writing, differing even in their mode of beginning and ending their letters. But both come over as wholly contented with their parents and their lives to date. Quite a number of my contributors wrote in similar vein: these two were selected as I wished to include an example of successfully *adopted siblings*. Martin's letter is more typical of the happy letters than is Keith's, most of the cheerful replies being fairly short.

As is clear from the accounts given in this chapter, the majority of the adoptees who replied have mixed feelings about their families and their early lives. In this, I think that they resemble the majority of people brought up by their biological parents.

IV
Viewpoint of Adoptive Parents:
Joys and Griefs

It will be remembered that the wording of my circular letter to adoptees differed from that used for adoptive parents. The former enquired ostensibly about "advantages and drawbacks", whereas the latter requested notes on the experiences of being an adoptive parent and, in particular, information about any problems that had arisen, directly or indirectly, as a result of adoption.

The majority of the parents replied in terms of joyful fulfilment at having finally achieved parenthood, of the great pleasure that their children have given them and continue to do, and of how much they would have missed if they had *not* had a family. Whilst this is important and good to know, it does not make for very varied or exciting reading! Hence most of this chapter is devoted to examples of those difficulties and problems which adoptive parents have met. If these appear to predominate over the joys, I must emphasise once again that the joys were frequently mentioned but were largely similar from family to family and therefore that spelling them out would have made for rather repetitive prose. But the setbacks were very varied and for this reason they are perhaps the more informative.

As in preceding chapters, I have tried to restrict my examples to problems that stem from the fact of adoption – although I am aware that this proviso may appear arbitrary and, in some instances, may indeed be so. Most of the difficulties that beset biological parents do also beset adoptive parents, but the converse does not hold.

Some of the problems are purely practical ones – though they may be none the less upsetting for that. For instance, Mr and Mrs Lime, parents of two adopted sons, Andrew and Hugh, say in the course of their letter: "Hugh, now aged twenty-three and married, was born in

51

one of the Dominions and adopted at the age of ten months . . . He had a jolt when, at the age of fifteen, he was taken to the Passport Office to get a juvenile document for travel abroad. The official, observing his place of birth in his short birth certificate, told him he was not a British subject. The man was soon disabused of this mistake, and we were glad that we had the 1956 Act to quote, being ourselves both British subjects; but the incident, occurring in the presence of other people, caused Hugh temporarily acute misery" – and hence, of course, acute and indignant misery on his account was suffered by his parents. Any indignity or hurt inflicted on an adoptee is experienced doubly strongly by his parents, who are liable to feel that an adopted child has enough to contend with in early life without unnecessary blunders from brash outsiders.

In some cases this may lead to a tendency on the part of the adoptive parent towards vigilant defensiveness. Several of my correspondents were evidently aware of the temptation to over-protect their children – perhaps to an even greater extent than biological parents. Thus Dr and Mrs Pine, whose adopted son is now married and in his early thirties, write: "Like any other only child Tony has suffered from some disadvantages, including the absence of a sibling-companion and probably, on occasions, parental love and concern carried to excess. This did not matter when he was young but may have been felt as suffocating when he was adolescent."

Again, Mrs Elder writes of her Dennis and Diana, adopted respectively at six weeks and ten days of age: "The principle on which we worked was the essential need to incorporate the children in a family unit, while at the same time making it very clear that they were adopted and not the children of the marriage . . . In our case, the result was to make them very 'special'. I now think that they were over-protected and that a little more rough and ready justice would not have done them any harm! They have both been late developers, which probably stems from the same source."

Mrs Birch wrote a happy letter in which she said how very glad she is that "we took the plunge thirty years ago and adopted a very bald little bundle with a torch of red hair" – five-week-old Tom, "who grew up to be the image" of his adoptive mother. A few years later they adopted Dorothy, who turned out very much like Mr Birch in appearance. Sadly, he died when Dorothy was still at school.

Problems were few and thought to be unrelated to the fact of adoption, e.g. Tom was dyslexic – undiagnosed, until the age of eighteen. Mrs Birch considers that his aggressive and hyperactive behaviour in childhood was due rather to his unrecognised dyslexia than to his adoption. He gained his Duke of Edinburgh's Gold Award, is very happily married (to a "darling girl who can spell!"), has a son and a daughter and is "a thoughtful and loving son".

The daughter, Dorothy, is also happily married. She was the easier of the two to bring up, although adopted at a later age. "She and I were very close," writes Mrs Birch, "but since she married she has been swallowed up by her husband's family and I feel a bit cast-off. However, if she's happy that's the main thing."

Three further points about the Birch family: "Dorothy and her brother don't really get on . . . Sometimes I think that my daughter would quite like to have been adopted by someone with money. She has always had very expensive tastes and likes beautiful things. She herself is a very beautiful girl and very fastidious. I think sometimes she finds me a little vulgar! . . . I am very grateful that I have a family. How much I would have missed without them."

The experience of the Cypresses with their adopted daughter again illustrates opposing tastes and attitudes – but in the reverse direction. Pamela was adopted at six months, and two months later Mrs Cypress "became pregnant with [her] son, Alan". There was thus a seventeen-month gap between the two children. In childhood, the main difference between them was that Pamela, despite a high IQ, did not progress well at school. "There have been two occasions on which she has had unkind things said about her being adopted but they did not leave any impression and she is wholly unconcerned about finding out about her antecedents. She seems to be quite happy about being adopted – we have always made happy stories about it – so much so that our son would write stories about himself when little and insisted on being adopted!

"There was the natural sibling jealousy, but years afterwards I was told she had once said, 'You can't tell me what to do, you are not my brother' – but *I* never heard anything like this." The parents' major disappointment, however, arose when Pamela was seventeen and she met a young man who "led her into his world. This consisted of embryo pop-stars and she has lived happily in this world ever since. Her friends have been chosen from the weaker and younger. I suspect she can thus feel slightly superior. There were no behaviour problems until she was eighteen, when she decided to live in the West Country near this boy and his friends."

She had several brief office jobs, was unemployed for a year and is now "again driving a van delivering groceries. At the moment she is in close touch with us as we are helping her with the purchase of a house, but she is a very independent girl, very straight about money matters, and never asks for anything. What I regret is the fact that the lovely years of getting to know each other on an adult footing never came and she has no 'family' instincts as she went almost straight from school into this alien society . . . Do not think that we do not love her for we do, but we are very disappointed that she has so rejected almost everything we stand for, including religion . . .

"We were told that the children were 'matched up' to adoptive parents, but we fear that apart from looks this was not so . . . I think basically it is just that we are disappointed at her attitude to life, which is so superficial . . . She seems to have rejected our standards and our way of life and our values. Our son, who was adequate though not brilliant . . . has emerged with a degree and a good job. He chooses his friends from the kind of people he has always mixed with and generally lives very happily by our standards . . . He and Pamela have not exactly 'hit it off' . . . I cannot help but feel she would have been happier with a family where no one expected anything of anyone and she could do nothing and no one would care. We may have tried to do too much. She certainly had a good education, but she made nothing of it. Her friends are chosen from the 'clubs and pubs' people; it can be somewhat difficult adjusting to them! I know she loves us and I feel we can do no more than accept her as she is . . ."

Several other contributors – some parents and some adoptees – have found that basic differences in life-style have caused regrets. Some decades ago this would have been described as differences "in social class", and it used to be considered as important to "match for class" as it was – and still is, in some quarters – to match for appearance. The emphasis on "class", with or without quotes, has changed over the years, however, for several reasons. Some deem it almost a dirty word and, as such, they avoid using it or thinking about it. Some merely consider it an old-fashioned concept – partly because the class-barriers are less high and rigid than they used to be and partly because generation-gap has to some extent superseded class-gap. And, perhaps most important in the realm of adoption, since class is expressed largely in voice, accent, taste and other conventions, it is generally thought to be an *environmental* rather than a genetic factor. Rose Macaulay's comment that with rise in social class, women's voices tend to deepen and men's to rise in pitch, is a shrewd observation, as true now as it was in the late 1920s, when her book first appeared.*

It is likely that tone of voice, in common with most traits that are not purely physical (such as eye-colour), is due to a combination of – and, indeed, interaction between – nature and nurture. Yet almost all who have had anything to do with adoption, as parent or adoptee or friend of the family, cannot fail to observe the gradual emergence of attitudinal differences in siblings who have been exposed to identical social conventions ever since their adoption in infancy. Such differences do arise also among biological siblings, but less frequently and less strikingly.

Two points on this topic occur to me. First, what I have called "conventions" are not always as trivial or superficial as the word suggests, nor do they concern only matters of snob value. Manners, for instance, are in the main a question of putting other people at ease – which may entail temporarily accepting *their* conventions.

In general, adoptees unthinkingly accept their parents' habits and manners *in childhood* but, in adolescence or adulthood, they may implicitly come to reject them, especially if their biological parents come from a very different background. In particular, their choice of companions and of idioms may become more and more divergent from those of their parents (as is seen in Mrs Cypress' account). When this phenomenon occurs in biological families, the change in behaviour is often temporary; it is liable to occur as part of the normal teenagers' expression of independence; and, when they reach adulthood, these young people will often embrace once again the values of their biological parents.

Secondly, this "reversion to type"– if it can be so designated – works in both directions. Phyllis Crabtree's account of her experiences of being adopted by someone less middle class than her biological parents, suggests that the malaise resulting from such disparity may well work both ways. Indeed, the prognosis for children adopted into homes "too high" in the social-cum-educational scale is probably happier than for children where the reverse is the case, since – if the adoptive parents have benefited from their longer, more intensive education – they should be more understanding,

*Rose Macaulay, *Keeping Up Appearances*, Collins, 1928.

more tolerant and better at controlling any display of disappointment at their adoptee's eventual way of life. The full narratives given in chapters III and V suggest that this is sometimes, but not by any means always, the case.

V

Selected Narratives from Adoptive Parents

Let us open this chapter with the Chestnut family. The Chestnut parents were one of the few couples that elected to answer my circular letter *jointly*: as will be seen in the letter that follows, the first part is written by Eric Chestnut and the second part by his wife, Brenda. As happens fairly frequently, Mrs Chestnut conceived, and successfully bore a child, after they had adopted – having been advised that they were unlikely to have any children born to them. It is of course possible that if they had *not* adopted, they would never have had a child born to them.

Dear Dr Heim,

My wife, Brenda, and I have been thinking about how to reply to your letter, and decided to share the writing of the reply. I hope this may be of some interest to you, but the whole history of our family seems to have been so smooth and uneventful that there does not seem to be anything very remarkable to report.

We were married in 1951 when I was thirty-nine and Brenda twenty-seven. After three or four years we were advised that it was unlikely we should have children of our own, and in view of my age we proceeded to try to adopt without delay. Nigel came to us at the age of six weeks in 1955, and Alison came at seven weeks in 1957. During that summer and autumn Brenda was seriously ill and had several stays in hospital, so that it was uncertain whether we should be able to keep Alison. At the end of October Brenda had an operation and made a good recovery and Alison's adoption went ahead in December. Brenda continued in good health and in the subsequent summer we were pleasantly surprised to find that she was pregnant, and Gillian was born in March 1958. Whether the operation had made it possible for her to conceive, or whether the two adopted children had made a difference, is uncertain.

As there was only three and a half years between the three of them the children all grew up together from babyhood, and as soon as they were able to understand, it became a family story how they all came to be our children. The policy was never to talk about another mother, but of the ladies who were unable to keep them, reserving the title of Mother or Mummy exclusively for Brenda. When Alison was a little girl at the village school another girl once said to her, "Your Mummy's not really your mother", or something like that. It did not seem to worry her much, but led to a discussion at home as to what a Mummy really is – the one who loves you and provides a home. As far as we can make out, Alison has never had any problems.

Nigel has a more anxious temperament, and seems to have felt insecure when we went abroad to Bahrein in January in 1966 leaving him with friends in England until he came out for the summer holiday in July. When he was about to come out to us, he asked his aunt (my sister) whether we might give him away as his first mother had done. She of course reassured him, but probably an important part of the trouble was that he had nowhere to call "home". After he joined us in Bahrein he seems to have had no more misgivings. He was boarding at Z School [name given] and came out to us for the Christmas holidays of 1966 and '67 and the summer holidays. We were in England on leave in the spring each year and came home finally in 1968, Brenda in July and myself in October.

Alison went to boarding school at X School, in Y [names given] after our first leave in May 1967, and Gillian joined her there a year later. Looking back now all three are glad that they went to these schools.

Neither Nigel nor Alison have shown the least interest in their original parents, having been ever since they can remember natural members of our family. Nigel is now twenty-five and not married, working near Evesham in Worcestershire at a farm shop, mainly concerned with growing fruit. Alison was married in September 1977 and lives with Patrick, her husband, in the Midlands. She has a secretarial job with the Open University. Patrick works for an engineering firm.

We asked Gillian if she had any particular point of view on the subject of having an adopted brother and sister. Her only comment was that it was an advantage to her, as otherwise she would have been an only child.

The following part of the letter is in Mrs Chestnut's handwriting:

As far as the process and problems of bringing up a "mixed" family is concerned I find it difficult to remember specific differences between adopted or "homegrown" children. Sometimes I wished that I had more insight into hereditary factors, if we were going through some "mini-crisis", believing at that time that this knowledge might have helped – but even in the case of Gillian whose antecedents I did know, I cannot say that that knowledge really helped me. Perhaps parents look too often at similarities between their children and past members of the family until the child is almost type-cast as it were, and cannot just be seen as himself.

I think that I consciously made an effort to provide maximum security in the home background, keeping in mind the fact that the adopted children had already experienced a traumatic incident in their lives. Despite their being so young, I am sure the whole incident of being handed over from one person to another, keeping in mind the emotional state of all adults directly concerned, must have some unsettling effect on the babies. I remember being quite worried when Nigel slept almost the entire time for the first few days and never cried – on reflection I consider that this could have been caused by shock. Alison cried almost continually for the first few days and would not be comforted.

Our departure to Bahrein without Nigel was very demanding on him and troubled me greatly at the time – but I felt that it was very important for my husband that we should go, and we had to trust to God that it was the right thing to do. Nigel benefited later in so many ways from our stay in Arabia that we all agree it worked out well.

School holidays were always set aside as very special times, when the family came together – to do things together and we as parents tried to spend the maximum time in family pursuits. This I am sure is where our family unity grew and now that the children are adults and away from home, this unity is reflected in their delight in gathering together in the family home and their great affection and friendship for each other, and this I am glad to say now includes our son-in-law Patrick.

Perhaps this all sounds rather self-satisfied, but I would be less than honest if I didn't admit that we are delighted with each one of our children – and have much happiness and joy in them.

We wish you every success with your book and hope that you can put right some of the mistaken ideas many people have about adoption. If in any way we can be more helpful please let us know.

Yours sincerely,
Eric Chestnut & Brenda Chestnut

The Chestnuts' story is a typical case of uncomplicated, very rewarding adoption. All the ingredients are there: a stable, adaptable, happily married couple, adopting two babies who turned out to be "well matched", and afterwards having a daughter born to them – herself glad not to be an only child and warmly accepted by her older brother and sister.

The following story is at the other end of the spectrum, illustrating an exceptionally complicated and difficult situation:

Dear Dr Heim,

My neighbour, Mrs Nora Spruce, passed on to me your letter requesting information concerning the experiences of adoptive parents. When I finally sat down to my typewriter I just bashed out the enclosed. It may not be of much value for your projected book but if you want to follow up any particular points I would be happy to respond.

If you have any ideas about Philip's taciturnity I would also be grateful.

Yours sincerely,
Douglas Cedar

re Philip Cedar. Born April 1967.

Our experience as adoptive parents differs from most (not all) others because Philip is our grandchild. We have two sons of our own: Miles (born in 1942) and Daniel (born in 1943). Philip is the son of Daniel and a woman named Carol, with whom he was living for a time.

60

The circumstances leading to our adopting Philip are as follows. After Philip was born Daniel and Carol came to live in our flat but after moving out in the summer they subsequently broke up and Daniel asked whether we (my wife and I) would help him bring up Philip as Carol wanted to put him in a Home. We agreed. At the same time, as Carol was an unstable character (she had had other children whom she abandoned) we thought it better for security if we adopted Philip. This involved discussions with the social welfare people of District X [name given] who were not particularly helpful.

Obviously, they thought we were not suitable adoptive parents because of our age (I was born in 1909, my wife in 1919). We would have been prepared for Daniel to become the adoptive parent but he preferred us to take that role. Just as well, possibly, because in October he suddenly disappeared without saying a word. Two days later we received a note from one of his friends to say that he had gone abroad "to think things over". We did not see him for a long time nor did we hear from him but subsequently he returned to England and made contact.

In the meantime, my wife and I went ahead with adoption proceedings and these were finalised in March 1968. Both my wife and I had full-time jobs, although I was often home during the day because once a week in four or five I worked night duty. We live in a second-floor flat with no garden and the physical difficulties initially were arduous. Life was not made easier because Philip was a fractious child, did not sleep well and did not make good progress physically.

My wife hired a nursery trained children's nurse who was probably too young for the job (she was twenty-one) and not sufficiently experienced. It soon became clear that Philip was a very bright child with a strong will and the nurse could not cope all that well. I helped as much as I could when I was home during the day and often relieved the nurse by taking him out for long walks, etc. My wife had a well-paid, satisfying job in a bank, but was not too happy about the situation so far as Philip was concerned. There were the sleepless nights allied to the fact that he was not putting on weight. In any case my wife was far more emotionally upset by the whole business than I was. First of all, initially she was not as fond of him as I was; she had resented the whole relationship between Carol and Daniel and considered Carol a bad mother; furthermore, she could foresee her entire life being disrupted. Being wise after the event, we should have engaged a far more mature, motherly woman to live in to look after Philip while my wife continued with her career but we didn't and my wife eventually gave up her job (including pension rights) to devote herself full time to Philip.

The change in him was immediate. He began to put on weight and sleep better. He developed into a bright, lively and articulate child. From then onwards there were no particular problems, apart from the normal ones of bringing up children (complicated, of course, by the fact that we were so much older than the parents of his friends). Philip of course did not realise at first that he was not our child, but our grandchild, but we told him early that he did not come out of his mother's tum but another lady's. This was not particularly difficult because there was a family living opposite with three adopted children (two of them twins about a year younger than Philip).

Complications developed when Daniel came back to England, married and had two children with his new partner. I have always taken the initiative in telling Philip of his background and I have to say here that my wife has not (and does not) always agree with me. In fact, it has been the basis of many arguments between us, probably lending support to the argument that "there are no problem children, only problem parents"! Indeed, I am sure she would give a different version of events but as she would not write to you about this in any case there is no point in developing this. Daniel and his wife lived a few miles away but we saw them from time to time. As we are surrounded by people who know the circumstances of Philip's adoption and his parents I felt it was necessary to inform him about his background before he learnt of it from other sources. This is the line I have always adopted.

The next step was to tell Philip that Daniel was his natural father. Daniel was not too happy about this. By this time he had a daughter and a son and his first response was "What is Miranda [Daniel's daughter] going to say?" That, I told him, was his problem! Maybe not too kind on my part, but Daniel has never been of help so far as Philip is concerned, either financially or otherwise. When it came to it, however, it was easy and both Philip and Miranda and her brother Simon were quite pleased to learn that they were half brothers and sisters. In any case Philip and Miranda (now nine) are very similar in many ways temperamentally and get on well.

When Philip was much younger I had told him that I was not

sure where his mother was (I believe she was in Africa at the time) but said that when he became older and wanted to meet her I would do my best to help. The next complication was when Daniel's marriage broke up and he went to live in Canada for about a year.

The position at the moment is that Daniel is back and we see him and Miranda (sometimes with Simon, sometimes not) about a couple of times a month for Sunday lunch. Superficially Daniel and Philip get on and seem to like each other, but obviously Daniel feels that Miranda comes first.

In the beginning of 1978 news came through that Carol had died in Berlin from a drug overdose (whether accidental or deliberate I don't know). I was for breaking the news to Philip but my wife strongly opposed so that it was not until about a year later I told him. "Well thanks for not letting me go to her funeral," he said. I explained that in fact no one from England so far as I know (not even her mother) went to the funeral. What has always worried me about Philip is that he never asks questions about his mother. On the other hand Miranda's mother tells me that Miranda is very curious about Philip's mother and often asks questions. Whether it is because little girls are more curious than boys I don't know. For instance, my wife has almost total recall about her childhood whereas I can remember only a few isolated incidents.

Some time back I came across an old snapshot showing in a group my wife's mother and father (now dead) and Carol. Carol was quite a pretty woman. I asked Philip if he knew who the group was. Of course, he knew his great-grandmother and great-grandfather. "And the young woman?" I asked. "Don't you know – That was your mother." He said, "Urgh!" "What do you mean 'urgh'?" I asked, "she is quite pretty," but he left it at that.

I have spoken about both Carol and Daniel to Philip from time to time but, as I have said earlier, he does not ask questions and rarely comments. Carol, unfortunately, had a rather chequered career and I want to protect Philip from the more sordid aspects of her life but I would prefer he learned the truth (if not all) from me than from gossip. So far as Philip's relationship with me and my wife are concerned it is of course not easy to be objective. I think my wife finds things more difficult than I do. She feels he does not love her but I think she is wrong. She is also rather obsessed by the age gap and that Philip is an only child. We have discussed this, of course, with other parents and friends and they also feel she is wrong. Naturally, we cannot help comparing Philip's attitude with those of Miles and Daniel when they were his age (Miles, incidentally, lives in Copenhagen and Philip, who was recently on holiday with him, probably gets on better with him than with Daniel; Miles in any case is far more considerate).

What younger parents tell us is that the present crop of twelve and thirteen year olds are a damn sight worse than a generation ago! There are the usual arguments, of course, about tidiness, cleanliness, homework, going to bed early, etc.

Philip is a talented boy but rather indolent. He plays the violin well, but could do better. He is in the top stream at a comprehensive school but could do better. There is no doubt that he is bright. Sometimes I have a feeling that children have recollections of before they were born, but maybe I am indulging in fantasies, but I must confess that I would be happier if Philip showed the same sort of curiosity as does Miranda.

He is a tall, handsome lad and resembles, of course, both my side of the family and my wife's in appearance. Kindly neighbours say we "have done a magnificent job" on bringing him up but both my wife and I realise others could have done better and no doubt we ourselves could have done better. But we did not have much choice in the matter, although faced with the same problem we would have done the same again, although probably a bit more intelligently.

As Mr Cedar states at the beginning of his saga, for a married couple to take on a young relative and bring up him/her as their adopted child, is not without precedent. But this story must be exceptional in the number of "slings and arrows of outrageous fortune" that have come the way of Mr and Mrs Cedar.

I shall let this particular narrative make its own point rather than attempt to moralise, in what would be an obvious and hindsightful manner. But I cannot refrain from paying tribute to the grandparent-parents for the their fortitude in the fact of ever-increasing problems and (insofar as this can be judged) for the objectivity with which the story is unfolded.

The factual approach, and the simplicity of style achieved by Mr Cedar, is in marked contrast to the following contribution, couched as it is in somewhat self-consciously "psychological" terminology. This letter was the second anonymous one that I received. I have named the writer Fiona Evergreen, as this is easier than referring to

64

her as Mrs Anonymous II, but I have adhered to her technique in designating her children by initial only and in the use of symbols such as "$^6/_{52}$" and "$^2/_{12}$", in preference to "six weeks", "two months", etc.

Dear Dr Heim,
　So sorry not to reply sooner to your letter, which we received several weeks ago. When attempting to put pen to paper we both felt increasing difficulty in thinking in terms of *problems* – or, more specifically, problems resulting from adoption. (I don't think (hope) we have (m)any blind spots!!)
　As an overall statement we feel that some problems may well arise from preconceptions and thereby victims of – either one's own or dealing with other peoples and the paradoxes thereof.
　We adopted K. (male) at $^6/_{52}$ being our 2nd "choice" (now approaching 16 yrs) being absolutely certain that he was "right" despite his howls. (The X Children's Society [name of Society given] and two very sensitive and intelligent Adoption Officers.) He always grew up with the knowledge – even from before he could understand what it really meant – and how glad we felt about it all.
　We successfully produced a fine girl three years later (I am diabetic and although very well did have a very bad history of childbirth). There was no problem of acceptance despite the fact that I was in hospital for $^2/_{12}$ but luckily we were able to maintain K.'s routine with the help of a friend or two, and, of course, extra involvement on my husband's part.
　As far as we were concerned "whose womb" was of little relevance – in fact as time went by K. seemed almost more interesting if anything as a "unique" individual, K2 (female) had very recognisable characteristics of ours!!
　We tended not to mention "the difference" except on occasions or in contexts where it seemed silly not to – a very large group of friends and relations obviously knew – and when we did mention it to new friends it was not in the hearing of either child. I found I always added the rider, "but it's an academic difference only", realising that this may be interpreted as a defence but feeling myself that the preconception of most people was that you *must* feel a difference.
　We have sometimes wondered whether the children were a little more physically boisterous with one another than is usual, but if this was so it seemed to be counterbalanced when one or other was

in "hot-water" when all the mutually supportive defence mechanisms were brought into play.

In relation to our preliminary statement it was interesting recently at a careers discussion to hear the suggestion of K.'s science teacher suggesting that perhaps K. should be encouraged more in this direction as job prospects were better. This teacher is someone we know fairly well and like very much. K. is intelligent and broadly based academically preferring creative English, language, art, etc., but being sufficiently intelligent to get reasonable marks in the sciences, although they are not his favourite subjects. Later we did mention that we knew that K.'s birthright father had discontinued his career as a medical student in favour of the Arts although his Mother had been a nurse, and so we felt that all options should be kept open, but—! The teacher's reply was, "Oh, I'd no idea he was adopted – I shall view him in a different light now"!!

(We are both very interested in the Arts, Music, etc. My husband read History at University and his career is involved in the human side of industry while I am medically based!)

K.'s original father was also Italian and this is able to be, and is, very positively accepted by K. We both have parents, etc., in Bath (Roman city) and one of my sisters lives in Verona so Italian food – holidays – language are available and enthusiastically taken up by K.

His comment recently when I did bring the conversation around to his birthright parents was – "but I never even knew them".

Well – I hope this isn't too rambling – all I can really say is that everything has been very straightforward for us indeed.

My reason for including Mrs Evergreen's letter *in toto* was mainly as an example of a six-page letter (the handwriting is large) that in effect conveys little information about the adoptee – though, incidentally, quite a lot about his parents. It is interesting, however, in that once again adoption was followed by pregnancy; that the schoolmaster felt that he should revise his view of the boy on learning that he was adopted; and that the parents claim "if anything" greater interest in K1 (adopted) than in K2 (their biological daughter). A comparable feeling is expressed by Mrs Forest, when comparing her adopted daughter Deborah with her biological daughter Valerie (see page 88).

The next letter is a sad one. Mrs Janice Lichen and I had vaguely heard of each other but we had not previously made contact. When I embarked on writing this book, a mutual acquaintance – aware of my search for adoptive parents – gave me Janice's name and address. I therefore sent her a copy of my circular letters and we have since become friends. Her reply was as follows:

Dear Alice,

Thank you for your letters – I should have written to you before this but time has been short and Christmas was extremely busy. I have fifteen minutes now so I will at least *start* a letter to you!

Not all the contacts I have were helpful – one lady who is quite a good friend of mine insomuch as she visits me once a week, at first said she would give a letter to her oldest son now thirty-five (adopted). She has a younger one thirty-three of her own. But when I actually gave her the letter she became furious and I got a very icy phone call, saying that she's decided she didn't want to drag it all up again. Her adopted son was one of twins. She had him soon after his birth and the loss of her own still-born child. It must have been an awful time for her – such as none of us like to re-live. She also said she didn't know if her daughter-in-law knew if her husband was adopted and she'd rather forget all about it. In view of this I didn't give her one of the letters for parents. I noticed too that Clive [Mrs Lichen's husband – now living elsewhere with another woman] was distinctly touchy and I don't know if he has replied.

A further friend in Southampton said she did not have the time to reply as she did a lot of voluntary work for the WVRS and it was like a full-time job. She did, however, comment in passing that she often wonders (now aged forty-five) what her real parents were like and if her three children have any of their characteristics. But she had never liked to ask her parents who had adopted her if they knew anything. To quote: "I still wonder about my origins and whether my mother might still be alive. Now that I have my own children, I wonder how much in their characters come from my side. However, one can always have one's fantasies which may be sorely dashed if one knew the truth!"

For myself I had a daughter of my own, who would now be twenty, who died two days after birth (toxaemia, blood pressure, caesarian operation and the baby had to be removed at seven months). With my son Colin, aged eighteen, I had all the same trouble, but he grew almost to full term before he was successfully removed. I was advised not to have any more children – it was pre-pill and abortion days and there were many children needing homes. We were asked to adopt two of the opposite sex [i.e. girls] as we had a boy. As Colin was red-headed, we were also asked to adopt red-headed children as they were generally not wanted as much as they were obviously adopted.

My son was very jealous and when older asked me why I wasn't content with just him. He has a good relationship with his youngest sister and has recently developed a careful relationship with the older one – this has been helped by the fact that he is a bass guitarist in a Pop band at weekends and the older girl gets reflected glory from this (!). So she has made an effort too.

Monica is fifteen and a half and Charlotte is thirteen. Both adopted at seven weeks. As a baby Monica was no trouble at all, but since her teens she has been nothing but! The past year has been the worst and I think the whole situation is aggravated by the fact we are now one-parent. "I can quite see why he left you," she says. She says she doesn't feel part of the family but always refuses to join in things, is out or very late for meals. This is partly because she has a horse and has to earn money doing paper rounds to keep it. She says she really hates me and swears like a trooper at me and we have come to blows – all of which is very wearing. I seem to work so hard on her behalf as I do the other two but it is hardly noticed but then I don't think parents are – children are really ignorant of what is done for them until it is their turn to care for others. She could be my husband's own daughter – so alike is their attitude! The relationship upsets me as naturally I want to be a good mother to her but I feel she won't let me.

Another adopted girl once said to me, "It doesn't matter how much you love her or what you do for her, you are not the right person doing it. She just hates you because her own mother didn't keep her."

In contrast to date my younger daughter is kind, considerate, loving, practical, intelligent and this in itself may cause just sister *vs.* sister trouble which is nothing to do with the adoption. I get depressed because I don't know how to cope with all the difficulties that confront me. At times I find it difficult to keep alive and then I'm glad they are not my girls as I would hate them to have inherited my tendency to depression.

I don't know if you would like to drive over for a meal one evening (a Wed. or Thurs. is my best night) and meet us all. It may

68

be of more value than this letter for you to see for yourself. Neither of the girls like it mentioned they are adopted – this feeling was very strong when they were ten to eleven.

If there is anything else you'd like to know, do get in touch.

Yours sincerely,
Janice

The depression evinced by Janice is evidently the result of lonely grief at being a deserted wife, plus the strain of coping with children-and-job, plus family clashes that are exacerbated by the fact that the daughters are adopted. It is, of course, the last with which we are primarily concerned – although the three aspects inevitably interact with one another.

Whilst it is possible that Colin might have been jealous if he had had two biological younger sisters, he would hardly have felt the same way about it – and would almost certainly not have expressed his feelings as he did. And whilst we all know of teenage girls (and boys) who are horrid to their biological mothers, it does look as though Monica consciously resents being an adoptee – in addition, perhaps, to scorning her mother for her failure to "keep her man". This combination must be bitterly painful for the mother.

One-parent families created by the voluntary desertion of either the father or the mother are often prone to conflict and tension, both of which may be heightened when one or more of the children are adopted. Feelings of guilt and disloyalty, failure and resentment, are intensified on all sides, resulting, quite often, in a vicious spiral.

The story of Mrs Quince, which follows, is very different since her Roger was adopted at two years of age, her family is united and the two older (biological) sons warmly welcomed Roger, from the moment he joined the family.

Dear Alice Heim,

I think it's best that I should reply on behalf of our son, Roger, and my husband and I since I can't see him ever getting down to putting pen to paper. He came home this weekend from boarding-school, so I managed to have a discussion with him.

Roger is fourteen years old, and was adopted at two years old. He had a Grade 3 systolic heart murmur. He was highly strung and had a violent temper, which traits he inherited from his mother.

It was extremely helpful to know this and other pieces of

69

information about his parents, as it helped us, for instance, to try not to let him get frustrated to flash-point too often since he felt (feels) things more than most, and his temper explodes beyond reason – then he feels utterly desolate afterwards. Nowadays he rarely loses his temper, though he cries more than most boys. Having been in the X Home [name given] he wasn't used to cars, fires, TV, men and so on, so he had much to get accustomed to.

We have two older sons (now aged seventeen years and eighteen years) of our own, who made Roger laugh and he immediately adored them. Any worries took the form of violent nightmares, when he scratched the walls like a demented animal, pulled curtains down and pulled tucked-in bed-clothes back. After many sleepless nights, when I showed him the stars, rocked him, talked to him and even smacked him, I finally sat down on the stairs with him and cried myself – that was the answer! He couldn't bear to see me cry, and thereafter I pretended to do so whenever he got out of control, and he's gradually learnt to forget himself and reach out to others.

He's really apprehensive of "being told off" and therefore worried about tackling anything new like cycling, being in the swimming team, etc., just "in case". Seeing a grown-up as vulnerable as he is, therefore, has given him confidence. Now he's at boarding-school and is, apparently, a tower of strength to a friend whose parents' marriage has broken up.

Right from the start we told him, in story form, of his being chosen by us – i.e., that there was once a Mummy and a Daddy who had two boys in the family, who all wanted a little boy with grey eyes, etc. (description of Roger) to come and live with them in their house. So they prayed that God would show them . . . etc. – story of search – until they went into the room of the big house, and there, sitting on the floor was a little boy with grey eyes and blonde hair – was . . . And Roger always finished it by a glowing – ME!

At about the age of eight years he started showing off too much about the fact that he was "special" and that his parents *had* to have his brothers and didn't *choose* them – So we had to pull him up short, and explain how everyone is special in their own way.

At about ten years the questions started cropping up like: "Why do you think my Mother didn't want me?" – and, "Do you think she liked leaving me?" . . . I used to explain that if there was a Mummy without a Daddy she didn't have a home, time, etc., but vagueness didn't suit.

I was advised by a lady who had found out in her late teens through an aunt that she'd been adopted and, even after knowing of that shock, her adoptive parents pretended that they didn't know who her real parents were. When she discovered that they'd lied to her on that score too, she hated them. She advised me to go straight home to Roger and tell him *everything* we knew about his real parents so he wouldn't build up fantasies about them.

This I did. It was in the middle of the spate of Irish jokes, actually, and when I told him his Mother was Irish, he was horrified and almost dismissed her in one wild thought! Having covered all the information we had of them, Roger hasn't mentioned or worried or even thought of them since.

Until he went to boarding school over a year ago, he was probably two years behind in emotional maturity. He won an art scholarship to Y [name given], which means he is much respected in that field. Physically he is all right now, though so far he is the smallest in his year. The hole in his heart healed up spontaneously at three years old (after we had had the laying on of hands and anointing of oil for him).

. . . Meanwhile, we wish you all success with the writing of your book . . .

With good wishes,

Yours sincerely,
Angela Quince

This narrative is interesting and instructive on the way in which Mrs Quince – supported by her husband and older sons – managed to cope with Roger's physical and emotional difficulties. There is much in this account that we have met before, notably the story told of "finding" or "choosing" the adopted child and the importance of telling him all that is known about his background as early and as fully as possible. But what is new and enlightening is the significance of Mrs Quince's admission of weakness to her young son, when all else failed. "I finally sat down on the stairs with him and cried myself – that was the answer!"

I am not suggesting that that is always the answer, or even that this would necessarily have worked if Mrs Quince had deliberately tried it earlier. It might well not have; and with some children it never would work. But I am suggesting that it is desirable sometimes to let our children, when young, see our weakness, our flaws, our ignorance and our vulnerability. If we constantly maintain an appearance of strength and virtue and omniscience, it can be rather dismaying for a child; the façade will not always fulfil its function, and, sooner or later, the child is bound to suffer great disillusion!

The next contribution is from Mr Roy Peach, who claims, quite convincingly, that his adopted daughters were – and remain – very happily integrated into the family and yet declines to pass on to them my circular letter for adoptees. His first letter reads as follows:

Letter I

Dear Dr Heim,

I am very sorry to have kept you waiting so long for a reply to your letter. The real reason is that I have become increasingly uneasy as to whether I could ask my daughters to help as you suggested. Probably had the request for information been in the more conventional form of a questionnaire, their reaction might have been more predictable: but I feel that the "open-ended" questions which the letter puts before them might have both worried and disturbed them – and one especially might have preferred that this particular sleeping dog should have been left comfortably asleep.

So I hope it won't be much of a loss if I don't pass on your request. If I say that I am sure they treat each other as "normal" sisters – or perhaps I should say that they are very friendly, confiding in each other and asking each other for advice – and that our relationship with them is affectionate and relaxed – you may wonder why I am reluctant to ask them. I can only say that I have an intuitive feeling that it *might* be better not to.

Anyhow, best wishes for the success of the book!

Yours sincerely,
Roy Peach

In my reply to this letter, I said that I understood how Mr Peach felt about passing on the Adoptee-letter to his daughters but that I should be very grateful if he would be kind enough to answer my Parent-letter. In reply, I received letter II plus the "comments":

Dear Dr Heim,

Herewith my comments, though I am afraid they won't be much use to you – or anyone else! It really does seem to me that such problems as we have met have been those common to most parents and children, rather than any peculiar to adoptive parents.

In fact, it is only such queries as yours that remind us that the children *are* adopted – the elder is now forty and we have got so used over the years to thinking of them as ours. And when all the children and grandchildren join us for Christmas it will seem even odder to think of them as in any way special.

Best wishes for Christmas and the best of luck with the book – please do not bother to acknowledge this.

Yours sincerely,
R Peach

Mr Peach's Comments

Two daughters: Diana adopted in 1939 at the age of a few weeks, and Joan adopted in 1945, also at the age of a few weeks.

Attitude of relations, friends, to adoption: (1939)

Father-in-law strongly advised against it, and ridiculed the idea ("taking on other people's problems"). Thereafter the children were ignored and never referred to in letters, or conversation – or at Christmas or birthdays.

They were puzzled by this, but not bothered – and when he, in his late eighties, came to live with us, they showed him every sympathy and consideration, looking after him when we went away for short holidays.

All other relations and friends treated them just as they would had they been our own.

Awareness of Adoption.

Diana knew about adoption through conversation from a very early age, and *The Chosen Baby** (then one of the few books dealing with it from a child's point of view) was, among other books, often read – by request – when she was three or four years old. From then on it was taken for granted and rarely referred to, and she did not

---

*Wasson, Valentina, *The Chosen Baby*, Oxford University Press, 1941.)

mention it to her friends. She was, however, very angry when, at her secondary school, unkind references were made about another girl because she was known to be adopted.

Joan's awareness of adoption seemed to be reached much more gradually, even though it was talked about in much the same way. When she was about eight, referring to my wife's breasts, she said, "You fed me with those, didn't you?" and only began to grasp the situation in the subsequent discussion.

Later, in her teens, she began to wonder about her mother – had she been poor, lonely, distressed – and when reassured about her present situation, was satisfied and said she didn't want to know anything more about her.

When, in their teens, they saw (on TV) an American film dealing with the situation where the "natural" mother turns up and tries to claim her child back, they were both outraged.

Adolescence.

There were, I believe, no special problems during adolescence that could be attributed to their being adopted, though there were many of the usual ones: Diana was amused to discover that some of her friends "natural" mothers could be just as angry, fussy, and exasperated with their behaviour, as we could.

I am sure it was reassuring for each of them to know that they were both adopted. When a cousin joined the family (owing to the death of her mother) this led to some problems of jealousy on the part of the younger daughter, then aged four, as the cousin and the elder girl tended to "gang-up" and leave the other one out of things. This problem eased when the younger girl became very friendly with a neighbour's daughter.

They both found suitable husbands and are happily married, with children they enjoy, and they keep in friendly and frequent contact.

On receiving Mr Peach's first letter I did realise, of course, that he hoped he had finished with his unknown and importunate correspondent. But I persisted because I had found, by that time, that the majority failed to reply at all and I hoped, too, to discover why he was unwilling to pass on my adoptee-letter, since his daughters were grown-up and evidently had a very satisfying relationship with each other and with their parents. I had earlier encountered a similar attitude on the part of several successful adoptive parents.

In the event, my persistence on this occasion proved worthwhile. Mr Peach's suggestion that his family had met no problems peculiar to adoption turned out to be wishful-thinking to some extent, in view of the initial reaction of his father-in-law, Diana's encounter with unkindness (to another adoptee) at school and Joan's occasional anxiety about her biological mother. These experiences are surely related to the fact of adoption.

On the other hand, it may well be best for an adoptive family if the parents do make the assumption of "normality" and do not dwell on problems that stem from adoption – provided they ensure that the basic fact is clearly recognised and accepted from an early age. This may be why several successful parents have preferred to leave "this particular sleeping dog comfortably asleep", as Mr Peach picturesquely put it.

The sympathetic acceptance by Diana and Joan of their recalcitrant grandfather in his old age, and the excellent relationship between them and their husbands and parents, confirm the satisfactoriness of these adoptions. Indeed, these relationships compare very favourably with those found all too often in biological families.

The next contribution differs from the previous ones in two respects. Mrs Holly, unlike the other adoptive parents, is not English. She was born and brought up in France and her spoken English has a markedly Continental flavour. She married an Englishman and they adopted a daughter, Rosalie. Mrs Holly, who is a music teacher, expressed her willingness to talk to me about the adoption but she declined to put anything in writing. She talked with great fluency – often so fast that I could not record it all: I was writing at full speed throughout the meeting. I put in an occasional question when she paused for breath. My questions are shown below, in brackets:

Mrs Holly's oral account

I'd like to *tell* you about Rosalie and her adoption . . . No, I don't want to write it. I'll tell you and you can write it down if you like. Rosalie is very happy to be adopted – she says that if she has no children of her own – you know she is married now? – she will certainly adopt – But she would adopt more than one. She often wished she had some brothers and sisters – she says she sometimes felt rather lonely.

I'll tell you something that could help – I always told Rosalie a little story from the age of two – how there were poor parents who were very sad indeed because they didn't have any babies . . . a sort of fairy story . . . and a beautiful blue shawl that the grandmother had wrapped up the baby in . . . and *we* were those parents . . . and *she* was the little baby girl . . . And she always wanted that story.

Another thing is a Special Day: we celebrate the day she was adopted . . . We treat her like a little queen – she is served first – and a beautiful dinner . . . no presents on that day . . . it's so much appreciated . . . make it important for the child.

(*How does she feel about being adopted?*) She couldn't care less – she's very proud of being adopted – she says if *she* can't have children she will adopt – but she will adopt more than one because she was sometimes lonely.

Oh, something else – rather sad – Rosalie was about eight and we were going to catch the bus and she suddenly said, "I've still got my Mother, have I? – She couldn't come and fetch me, could she? – I wouldn't want to go with her – I hope she's dead" . . . And some years ago when it was announced that adopted children could get in touch with their natural parents she said, "I *don't* want to know them – I want nothing to do with them." You see, *we* are Papa and Mama . . .

She had already adopted our ancestors – I've often told her that nobody failed, morally, in the family and that she never must. She adopted her grandparents – they took her to museums and that . . . It is *her* grandfather for her – her French cousins *are* her cousins . . . Rosalie is very artistic, you know, and my Papa said – he loves music and paintings – he said she is the one who is most like him.

(*Does Rosalie still play the piano?*) Yes, she does still play . . . They have a flat over her mother-in-law and *she* won't have a piano . . . But Rosalie won't lose her fingers . . . Gordon, my husband is retired from the Ministry of Agriculture . . . Yes, I used to teach music but we are both retired now . . . It was a nightmare . . . We have a picture of an ancestor – in French history . . . and she said she would have the portrait. . .

She reproaches me for just one thing – to have adopted only one . . . she has been very lonely. She says she wouldn't adopt only one – "Why did you adopt only me?" . . . *She* would adopt two or three . . . She reproached me many times . . . But she has a lot of cousins in France . . . in fact she gets on better with the French cousins than with the English.

(*How old was she when you adopted her?*) She was thirteen months old – that was too old – I think that's why she's so attached to home – because of security . . . I suppose the Mother wanted to keep her . . . We had great difficulty in getting the papers . . . So the *brother* signed the papers . . . Later we had difficulty with the passport . . . We are Catholics . . . the birth certificate is done – it says "adopted daughter of Mr and Mrs Holly" . . . Can get a baptism certificate in the name of the new parents – it says just "daughter of Mr and Mrs Holly" – *not* "adopted" . . . It took five months before the adoption went through.

(*After you had decided to adopt – did it take a long time?*) We had to wait two years – and we were very near the age limit – I had prayed quite a lot . . . then we saw a letter which said "a little girl, three months old" . . . but she wasn't suitable . . . we wanted an artistic or musical child . . . They came round – and they saw the piano – said, "Who plays the piano here?" . . . She was only two when I heard her singing the *Consolation* of Liszt . . . and she went easily from one key to another – her ears were there.

(*Do you know much about Rosalie's natural parents?*) No, the only thing we know – the Mother was convent-educated and she was a secretary. We never told Rosalie that . . . but she never asked about that . . . But she has a very good job, with her four languages – Daddy said that would be safer than music . . . She does secretarial work . . . English, French, Italian and German . . . But she will qualify in music and will teach music – when Bernard has finished with his Law qualifications . . . She would give a few lessons in the evening and get some pocket-money – It's nice to be independent with money.

If the Mother knew her daughter would be a good little girl, she would be pleased . . . Rosalie said one day, "Am I illegitimate?" and I said, "I don't know much about these things."

One day [at this point Mrs Holly lapsed into French] Rosalie was in the bath and Bernard, her husband, came into the bathroom – and Rosalie told me about it – she said she felt embarrassed . . . She says sometimes she'd rather be at home – I tell her home is where your husband is . . . Rosalie likes having French cousins – it's very pleasant to go to France and stay with them . . . She interpreted once at the age of five – at a garage . . .

(*Ever been any problems?*) Well, coming back late sometimes – and we would get worried . . . I remember one time she was out with some students – she was having coffee with them – so we went to the address . . . She said they were playing cards – it was one in the morning . . . She came back by taxi at two. We told her we were terribly worried and she said, "I didn't realise you'd be so worried – we were just playing cards – we were taking coffee." I said that two-thirty was too late . . . I said it should be midnight – so we compromised at one-thirty . . . We always sent a taxi for her . . . She was very considerate and often she phoned . . . We had to go and fetch her, wherever she was . . .

When she came to us, the social worker said she must sleep *alone* – not sharing a bedroom with her adoptive parents . . . So we did and she cried – she had been used to sleeping with several other children . . .

The interview ended abruptly when Mrs Holly suddenly realised the time: she had warned me that she could only spare about a quarter of an hour, though, in the event, she generously gave me longer. I include her contribution partly because it is the only oral one that I received and partly because it confirms a number of points made by other parents: the solitariness of the adoptee who is an only child, the fairy-tale quality of "the telling", and the moment of truth (or untruth) concerning the question of illegitimacy. On the other hand, it is more repetitious than most and more concerned with reassurance and self-reassurance.

We shall end this chapter as Chapter III was ended, with the Rosewood family. It may be recalled that the adopted sons, Martin and Keith, both wrote cheerful letters, in their very different styles, about their full enjoyment of life as children and as young adults. They had no reservations. As Keith engagingly put it: "I'm very happy with what I am, and those around me." Both parents wrote in similar vein and their respective letters are given below:

Dear Dr Heim,

Thank you for your letter of 11 February. My wife and I have talked over the request it contains, and have also discussed it with our elder son, Martin, who lives at home. We should be prepared to reply to the respective letters if you would be willing to give us a little time – a deadline is always a good idea, but from now until

Easter is one of my busiest times of year . . .

I hope we shall be able to help your book in due course.

Yours sincerely,

Victor Rosewood

Dear Dr Heim,

At last I settle down to try and answer your letter to adoptive parents. My husband and I have decided to answer separately and I do not know what he is writing. We have two adopted sons:

Martin Rosewood – born August 1956 and adopted at six weeks old.

Keith Rosewood – born March 1958 and adopted at eight weeks old.

When we received our first baby my husband and I were in our mid-thirties, had been happily married for four years (a first marriage for both of us) and had no biological children of our own. We adopted through a registered Adoption Society in Scotland and a good deal of information about the background of the two children was given to us by the Society. By the time that the boys were seventeen years old, everything that we knew was also known to them. This information had, of course, been given in easy stages, but they knew they were adopted by the time they went to nursery school at four. I purposely used this word from the start so that they were aware of it and had heard it from us first of all. In the very early days the story recounting how we had travelled from London to Aberdeen to fetch them back in an aeroplane proved a great attraction and had to be repeated very frequently when bathing them.

We never hid the fact of their adoption and in the early days I introduced them as "our *adopted* sons". When we returned from a five-year spell in Switzerland in 1966 (the boys being then ten and eight) I asked them what they felt about this. They were due to attend a new school and obviously many introductions would be made. Both said they preferred that the adoption should not be stressed as "we know we are adopted and it's no one else's business". From then on they used their own judgment over telling new friends and acquaintances.

I feel that we have been very blessed over our two boys, who have not caused us any real headaches. I have had friends whose children have been on drugs, were hippies, vanished, or simply remained at home and were unpleasant, and I know what a heartache all that can be.

Our elder son, Martin, found concentration very difficult and went through two periods of "non-achievement" in his work. At the time of his O-levels he had been at school in three different countries and educated under three different systems – Swiss, Scottish and English. He was a gentle and somewhat shy boy and each move was pretty painful for him although he always settled happily after a few weeks. His headmaster did not think he would get more than one O-level, if that. I did not know how far to be tough and push him, but decided to encourage and give him a good deal of my time if he wanted to chat or unburden. In the event he got his O-level, 3 A-levels, and graduated last year as MA of St Andrew's University.

Keith was more intellectually able and always very highly motivated. He sailed through all schools, picking up prizes and glowing reports and graduated with an honours degree in History from Cambridge, last June.

Both boys are very good friends and seem genuinely fond of each other, although their life-styles and choice of partners differ widely. Neither boy seems concerned to discover more about his background than we (through the Adoption Society) were able to provide, but I realise that with marriage in the near future this may change. Neither boy has, as far as I am aware, shown any desire to trace their biological parents.

I think that my husband and I have enjoyed bringing up our sons and have not worried unduly about being unable to produce a child. Having worked on the case committee of two Adoption Agencies, I realise how very painful this situation is for many couples.

Finally, I would like to say how much pleasure I have had from my two sons, how much they have contributed to family life and how much I have learned from them. I hope I can be a good mother-in-law to their chosen partners and I look forward to being a grandparent in due course.

Yours very sincerely,

Juliet Rosewood

P.S. I would very much like to know when your book is published.

The Adoption of Martin and Keith Rosewood
M.D.L. Rosewood, born August 1956
K.S.N. Rosewood, born March 1958

My wife and I were both over thirty when we married, and after four years it seemed probable that we should have no children of our own. We talked over the question of adopting children carefully together as has been our habit, and were in agreement about it. We both thought that we should adopt two children, and we both thought that they should be boys. We were fortunate in that in 1956 it was possible to adopt healthy babies – also that a good Adoption Society existed in the place where we lived and where my wife's family was well-known. I do not ever remember resenting the fact that the children were not my own. It seemed to me important that they should be Scots, and we flew twice from London to Aberdeen to collect our children!

It may be material to mention that there are other adopted children in my own family: in my generation, my sister (married at thirty-nine) already had two; and in the next generation, my nephew and his wife have two. I think we are "child-minded". I myself was the youngest of a "natural" family – born when my mother was forty-six – and had a very happy home and upbringing.

It seems that in twenty-four years we have had a smooth passage with our children, and have been a very united family – perhaps all the more so because we have had many moves in connection with my job and have lived in Scotland, England and Switzerland, with corresponding changes of school. The most difficult time we had with Martin (the elder boy) was over his primary schooling in Switzerland, where his performance was very poor, but when we returned to this country, there was a marked improvement. It could have been a problem that he is less clever, less athletic and less highly motivated than his younger brother, but he seems to have little jealousy in his make-up. We sent them to different schools from the ages of fourteen and twelve respectively. They had had different interests, friends, and life-styles, but have remained on good brotherly terms with one another.

I am very thankful to have such good sons – thankful to God and to my wife – and enjoy their company (in moderation, like most fathers), now that they are grown-up. Looking back, I regret the fact that having virtually no manual skills, except that of driving a car, I was unable to impart any to them, or to do much in the way of

81

sharing sports or hobbies with them. I don't think the younger boy, Keith, was impoverished by this since he has his own talents and the will to develop them, but Martin has probably grown up more useless than he should have done because of my limitations. Secondly, I am rather disappointed at my own lack of practical interest in their studies (I never used to help with their homework, for example), which might have been expected from someone who is supposed to be "intellectual". Of course I could plead to pressures of an absorbing job, and in a way I think it was a good thing that my wife took much more responsibility and interest in the children's "careers", since my job in any case tended to take over in our lives. A better balance has been preserved in this way, but I still suspect a fair amount of paternal selfishness! Perhaps the other side of the coin of detachment is that I have very seldom been angry with the children (though just as irritable as anyone else) and we have had hardly any rows in the family.

It was a great joy to me that Keith went to my old college, but I never insisted (even if it had been financially possible) that either of them should try for the public school that I attended. More important, it is also a joy that one son at least shares our Christian faith and *may* in the fullness of time seek ordination. With true British reticence we have discussed this very little, and only at his prompting.

Now we are thinking a bit nervously about our future daughters-in-law (much as we like them both, in their very different ways), and I look forward tremendously to being a grandfather, though I may not turn out to be a great success when it actually happens!

V.A. Rosewood

My reason for closing this chapter with the Rosewoods is partly because they were such a co-operative family – the only one of which four members made independent contributions. This seems to indicate an exceptionally deep sense of security on their part: none of them felt reluctant to awaken this sleeping dog. Again, several members felt relaxed enough to be able to indulge in a little dry humour. We have already commented favourably on Keith's frank expression of self-satisfaction. His father's humour took the form of a kind of mock-modesty, e.g. enjoying the company of his grown-up sons "in moderation, like most fathers", and admitting to "a fair amount of paternal selfishness". Many adoptive parents feel, even after years of experience, too uptight to recognise, let along admit to, such failings – if failings they be.

Finally, the family might not have had such a smooth passage (to use Mr Rosewood's phrase) if the parents had shown less wisdom and patience and had been a less united couple. Some potentially trouble-making seeds were there: the marked difference in gifts between the two boys and the frequent long-term travelling demanded by Mr Rosewood's work – these might have caused problems if handled less ably. Their story suggests the kind of home background in which adoptees are likely to thrive: enduring harmony between husband and wife, willingness to adopt at least two children and preparedness to steer the middle course between the Scylla of rigid regimentation and the Charybdis of over-indulgence.

VI
Coloured Adoptees

This chapter deals with a rather specialised topic: the deliberate choice of adopting non-white children. Some years ago, this would have been considered so eccentric a course that the inclusion of the topic would probably have been deemed quite unjustified. In case anybody should think this an over-statement, I should like to quote from a letter that I received in 1957 from the Social Worker who had aided me (after many ifs and buts) to find a baby girl. At that time I was eagerly seeking a brother for her. The Social Worker wrote: "The Committee was asking about a baby boy for you recently, but we have been most unfortunate. I went to see two last month on your behalf, but they would not have fitted in with you and your daughter. One had a Malay father and the other an American of doubtful colour. Of course they did not tell me this before I set off on a long journey to see them. *Needless to say, I did not accept them for anyone*" [my italics].

Not all potential adopters took the same view as the official adoption organisations even in the 1950s. But nowadays some would-be adoptive parents expressly request a black or yellow child or one of mixed race. This is partly because – with improved methods of contraception and easier abortion laws – the supply of traditionally adoptable infants has decreased and people who desperately want a child just *want a child*, regardless of its antecedents.

Some white couples, however, actively want a coloured family for more positive and specific reasons. Three of my contributors exemplify this position: the Forests, the Copses and the Woods. I quote each of their narratives in full, as all are interesting in their separate ways regarding adoption – and also as illustrating the attitude of the so-called civilised world to coloured children. We begin with Mr and Mrs Forest, whose story is particularly impressive:

84

Dear Dr Heim,

Your letter was passed on to me by Betty Conifer, who is a friend of ours. She thought I might be able to give you some information for your book on bringing up adopted children, and I will be very happy to do so. I'll list the children we have, and then, if you would like to know more about them, please telephone me, as there are so many it would take ages to write about them!

Yours sincerely,
Daphne Forest

		Date of birth
Graham	born to us	April 1963
Deborah	adopted Indian	December 1964
Trevor	born to us	July 1965
Frank	adopted Pakistani	July 1967
Valerie	born to us	October 1967
Heather	adopted African	March 1971
Julian	adopted African	March 1972
Isabel	mixed race, fostered with view to adoption	February 1976
Matthew	West Indian, fostered with view to adoption	August 1976

We had Deborah when she was twenty-one months old – very difficult child.
Frank was two and a half years old – easy
Heather was three and a half years – easy
Julian was two and a half years – easy
Isabel we had in June last year – had been badly treated and lots of foster-homes
Matthew we had at twenty-three months – gorgeous, but dreadful temper!

I wrote in reply to this letter:

Dear Mrs Forest,

Thank you so much for your letter and enclosure. I am of course deeply interested in your wonderful-sounding family. From my point of view the mixture of "biological" and adopted children is no less fascinating than is the mixture of nationalities.

85

I can well imagine that you are far too busy to write at length about each child. But it would be invaluable if you could possibly set down the problems that you have encountered in bringing up your adopted (and fostered) children: that is, problems that have arisen with them and *not* with the children born to you. I realise, of course, that in the case of your family, one cannot distinguish between problems arising from the fact of adoption (if any such exist) and those arising from questions of race, colour, etc. (if any such exist). But you do seem to be in a uniquely suitable position to attempt this.

I am extremely grateful to you for your willingness to co-operate.

With every good wish to you all,

Yours sincerely,
Alice Heim

Mrs Forest's generously long reply to my letter is given below:

Deborah

It was only after a long period of waiting that the X Childrens Society [name given] said that they had a little girl for us to foster with a view to adoption. We were told to see her, and then visit regularly for several months before bringing her home, but in fact it didn't work out like that.

Graham was nearly three and a half years, and Trevor was only just over one year, when we first visited Deborah – Priscilla as she was then called. Although we had asked to see her playing with the other children, so that she wouldn't suspect our interest in her, we were shown into a playroom – empty of people – and the little child was led in by the uniformed matron, and we were then left together. Deborah was nearly twenty-one months old, slim and brown, with cropped black hair and a very sullen face. My husband, Peter, warmed to her at once, but I didn't – she looked so wary and sulky, and so very unresponsive. She ignored us, and just sucked a huge padlock off a chest in the room. Later on, she did sit on my lap and looked at my purse, taking some coins out, giving them to Graham, taking them back and putting them back into the purse. The only thing she said was, "Ooh, look." I left the purse with her when we went home.

The next week we went to the Home again, and again were "given" the child by the Matron. This time the nurse who "specialed" Deborah came and said would we like to go to the park with her and Deborah, and we were pleased to see how quiet and well-mannered the nurse, Jenny, was – very calm and pleasant. She never spoke at all sharply when D. ran away or wouldn't put her coat on, and when she had a terrible tantrum she just sat and held her, for ages.

On the next visit the following week, we went into the garden where all the children were playing – D. quite by herself and not mixing. Soon after we arrived she began screaming, and screamed for most of that visit. She never talked to us at all, and we wondered how long it would take for us to get to a more friendly relationship. We were amazed when the Matron said, just before we left, would we take D. with us for good next week, as she was so difficult when we went and wouldn't settle to sleep and had to be put in a room by herself. We agreed and the next week, we took D. home. She was dreadfully sick in the car, but didn't cry at all – no one saw her off and all she was given was the dress she was in and three old dolls, which she would never look at. We did have her "routine" typed out – a frightening list of "get up, pot, wash, prayers, pot, wash, breakfast, pot, wash, play, pot, wash, lunch, pot, wash", and so on all day.

At home D. would not play, she just stood around. She didn't want cuddles, she couldn't kiss, she couldn't choose what she wanted on her bread and butter, wouldn't ask for the pot but went to order; she ate what she was given and slept well, but she just wouldn't respond to any of the ways in which we tried to get her stimulated. She seemed very old, not like a little tiny toddler – she was terribly fussy when she ate that her fingers were clean, and she wanted to be able to dress herself, and she soon managed. I remember how for some months she would never put her shoes on the right feet, no matter how I tried – she would always change them slowly and deliberately. She never laughed or cried with tears – if she fell over she cried with a queer noise.

I never felt close to D. for a long time. I had read Bowlby* and how he said that the first years were so important that a child adopted later couldn't make a good relationship with anybody, and D. was so reserved and unapproachable that I think I was

*Bowlby, John, *Child Care and the Growth of Love*, Penguin, 1952.

terrified that he was right and my theory that enough love would put anything right was wrong. Deborah seemed like a child wrapped in a plastic bag; you could see her and feel her, but not know her. She didn't fit in my arms or my heart because I think now I was too anxious that she should love me and was frightened that she gave nothing. I didn't realise then that she couldn't give what she hadn't got, and that my giving was really selfish, since it was aimed to get a response for my own satisfaction.

All this time I had been very gentle with D. – at the Home we'd been told that no smacking, no punishment was given, and D. did so little on her own that she wasn't ever naughty, just sullen. Then one day I had been watching her through the window – she was standing in a room full of toys, with Graham and Trevor playing near, and she was just standing. I couldn't bear it any longer and just went in and shook her and said "play" and gave her some bricks. She didn't cry, but she looked startled – the first change I'd seen in her eyes. I felt dreadfully guilty, but from then on I treated her the same as the boys – I no longer was extra-loving or patient – if she didn't respond when I spoke I got cross, and if she didn't take food when it was offered instead of putting it on her plate I didn't give it. I left a potty nearby but didn't put her on it. I felt mean and hard, but after a bit D. started to respond and gradually became much more "normal". She still had long bouts of extreme sulkiness when told off, and began to have periods of doing the most she could to annoy me, but at least it was better than doing nothing.

I became pregnant and gave birth to Valerie, and it was from then on that D. started to really become a person. Without being told she would fetch the baby powder, etc. and soon began to put the little clothes to warm before fetching them. As Valerie got older and more mobile, so Deborah got more and more responsive, and although the periods of intense sulkiness still came, they became less and less frequent, until they went altogether at about eleven–twelve years of age.

Deborah suffered a lot at school because of colour, and I think this had led to a lack of self-confidence. She knows, and always has done, that we chose her because we wanted her "a little old Indian", as Graham lovingly called her when he saw she was "brown all over" the first night she came home. She is very beautiful now, and is closer to me than Valerie in all ways. She knows what I am thinking, and we often laugh because she has done something I'd been thinking of doing. I feel so guilty about the first years – if only I'd realised all the mistakes I was making. My husband was much better – he just loved her for herself, and that was what I hadn't learnt to do, I just kept wanting her love for myself, and it wasn't until I stopped treating her as "different" and "special" that I really began to relax enough to wait for whatever came.

We never had any problems with the relationship of the children to each other – never have we had any jealousy from born or adopted children for the new ones as they came along.

Frank

When Deborah was about four and a half we took her back to the Home to show the matron and also to ask for another little boy – a baby Chinese if possible! The matron said she had no baby, but a two-year-old Pakistani boy was available for adoption. We said no, we weren't interested; but anyway we were asked to say hallo to the children. There, sitting on the floor, was a very fat little boy with the most beautiful eyes in the world, and he looked up and said, "I's doing to seep in a bid bed tonight." I knew at once that it was my son Frank sitting there (his name was Normal Aktah, and he was the two-year-old Pakistani), and so we began the agonizing fight to adopt him.

As he was only two months older than Valerie we were told it wasn't "their policy" to let a child go to a home where there wasn't a gap of at least nine months as it wouldn't be a "natural family"! That was only one battle. We were also told that five children were "too many", and what would we do when they were teenagers?! After five months of writing, going to London, etc., we won, but it still took some years before he was legally adopted. We never had any problems with Frank, as he fitted into the family as if tailored specially for it. He lacks concentration in some of his written academic work, although he is quite intelligent verbally, but I can't think that this problem is just because he was adopted, as I have found it quite common with other "born" children at school. He was teased at one school because of his colour, but he coped very well and it didn't seem to upset him as it has upset Deborah. Really, I cannot find any problems which have arisen because he was an adopted child. (I forgot to say that he is an asthmatic child, and reacts to cats, and some flowers, etc.)

89

We wanted to adopt another little girl, but couldn't get one of any sort from any adoption society. We did try to get a child from abroad, and wrote to many countries and went to see various Embassies in London. Still we couldn't get a child; and then we were told to try the London Boroughs. At last we found people who didn't react with horror at the idea of adding to our family of five, and who didn't try to make out we were odd to like having adopted children. After being accepted we soon had a phone call – they didn't like to suggest it, but would we take a brother and a sister, instead of just a girl? Of course we were overjoyed, and rushed to Bournemouth to see two lovely children, half Nigerian and half Ghanaian, the boy two and a half and the girl three and a half years old. After two or three visits they came home, and have been a delight always – they are eight and nine years old in March.

Heather is very placid most of the time but, very rarely, shows a terrific temper when roused. I cannot, again, find any problems which have arisen because she is adopted. At my school she does not get teased because of her colour, and she is popular with all her class-mates, and she gets on well with her brothers and sisters, being specially good with her new tiny sister. Sometimes she can be aggravatingly slow in things, taking life too calmly! But I'm sure this is just Heather.

Julian is a dear little boy – he amuses himself for hours and yet can join in family games, etc. He also has an amazing temper, but very seldom uses it. He is quicker in his movements than Heather, and cries easily if told off. He is suffering at the moment because he is finding school work hard – he reverses words and seems to lack the ability to retain things, like tables, in his mind. We are now having him assessed at a child clinic, because the others in his class are working so well that the gap in attainment is getting too great, and he is becoming more aggressive towards certain children in his class, being conscious of their greater ability to write things down. Verbally, Julian is good; his vocabulary is excellent and he asks intelligent questions. Again, I think these problems are just his problems, not arising from adoption.

Matthew

Matthew is West Indian – we have had him nearly two years, and he will be four in August. He is a huge boy, being very strong yet being very chesty and asthmatic. He came from the same Home as Heather and Julian, and we hadn't intended to have another child, but the matron rang us up and explained that the Home was being closed (a dreadful pity as it was such a good one) and wouldn't we like a very chesty but very forward twenty-one-month-old boy? She had loved him since he went to the Home as a new baby, and desperately wanted him to be loved. We of course said we'd come over, and went to Bournemouth again. Matthew was a very demanding, bad-tempered child who had an overwhelming and utterly loveable character – he was covered in scabies and eczema, and looked awful, but we knew he was ours and after one more visit he came home.

He had got the most violent temper when frustrated, and still has a few tantrums, but not nearly as [many as] he did the first year we had him. He is very bright and has a strong, unusual, and very loveable personality, being most affectionate and sensitive underneath his quite tough exterior. I cannot think of any problems which have arisen because he is adopted.

Isabel

We had Isabel last June. She is a bit older than Matthew, being four in February. Again, we had her by "accident" – a friend, who had a fostered boy very much wanted a little girl to foster (both with a view to adoption). She was found a tiny three-year-old who had had about seven homes and been badly treated in one, and was thought to be backward. However, her husband couldn't take to the child because she was partly coloured, and they were going to send her back into care, when we said we'd like to have her. After some negotiation it was agreed, and now she is a lively, attractive, really gorgeous little girl, and has been found to be average in ability. She, like Matthew, is much loved by her older siblings, and is no trouble – more than expected mischief! –at all.

I am afraid none of this will be of any help – I've tried to think about problems arising from adoption but can't – the main problems have been because of colour and lack of concentration in school work, these problems being much lessened because the children are all in my school – which I began for them.

Daphne Forest

Mrs Forest is clearly an exceptional woman. Apart from her inexhaustible supply of affection, patience, drive and faith, she has taken on a mixed family of nine children (mixed in every sense). She and her husband have full-time jobs: he as a clergyman and she as a headmistress of a successful school which she started for the benefit of her adopted children.

Thus the Forests can scarcely be described as a "typical family" with coloured adoptees – although the number of smaller families of this kind is gradually growing. Nonetheless, the Forest story is an instructive one, both in its triumphs and its problems. And it suggests that if more couples adopted coloured infants for choice, and nurtured them with the same understanding and loving care that the Forests have shown, the (primarily social) problems might diminish over the years. This would benefit the community as a whole, as well as the adoptees.

Desmond and Jill Copse's contribution follows. As will be seen, this is in the form of a report rather than a letter:

Mr and Mrs Desmond Copse, Derbyshire

Natural children: KENNETH (12), IRIS (11)
Adopted at age of six weeks: DAVID (9), SOPHIE (7). Mixed race: half Indian/English, both.

1 There was no problem in integrating the two babies into our nuclear family. We have never differentiated between our own and the adopted children. We were able to love them as our own from the word go.

2 Acceptance by the wider family wasn't so easy. The paternal grandparents strongly disapproved (particularly of the boy, who would of course carry on the family name). The maternal grandparents were suprised but supported us. Now both sides accept them as far as we can tell.

3 Environment: a country village, pop. 450. The adoption society needn't have worried about the "colour" thing, as people have been generally accepting. We were already accepted ourselves in the village community.

4 Playschool: three–five years. Both children (very attractive and normal) were readily accepted and had educative value as other children asked, "Why is David a brown boy?"

5 School: both were slower to settle in (despite being just round the corner) than our natural children. Though bright in personality

and articulate, they have been slower in academic progress than the other two. We think they have become more sensitive to their skin colour (rather than adoption) and possibly get teased by peer-groups. "Nig-nog" was a nickname one of them came home with, and even the odd "Paki". The nine-year-old finds it hard to concentrate for sustained periods in class and is probably emotionally insecure.

6 Personalities: both are particularly loving but quite happy to be independent of us and go to play with friends, parties, etc. They have never been "clinging" children, nor have our older ones. The seven-year-old girl was a very easy and contented baby, and has grown up to be an outgoing, attractive and good-natured child.

The nine-year-old boy is a more tempestuous character, as he was at six weeks old. He has quite a mercurial temperament. We believe that he was unwanted during his mother's pregnancy. After the birth, she couldn't decide whether to have him adopted or not (even when he was placed with us for the three months prior to adoption). We suspect this has left its mark in the emotional insecurity and lack of concentration he shows at school. He is a great home-lover.

Significantly, we believe that the little girl was always a "wanted" baby, as the mother had not been able to have children within her marriage.

7 Our own attitudes: possibly we feel more protective towards these two than our natural children. We anticipate new problems will arise during teenage years, specially over boy–girl relationships and their parents.

Present family problems which arise are no different from other families with four children living on a small income. As an ordinand in training for the C of E, I face a low salary for several years to come; I had previously been a public-school teacher for seventeen years.

One reason for adopting was the recent purchase of a rambling four-bedroomed house with large garden; we felt we had both space and love to share. As the population explosion was in vogue in the early '70s, we had decided not to have more natural children.

As we are both believing Christians, we expect the Lord to help us with any problems that come up. We say prayers with the children each night and hope they will find their own faith in due course.

Addendum:

Both know themselves to have been adopted, and so do the other children. We have simply tried to deal naturally with it when the subject has come up: emphasising, for instance, that they were specially chosen by us, etc.

We meet here, once again, the censuring attitude of some grandparents towards adoptees, exacerbated in this case by the fact that the children are not white – "The paternal grandparents strongly disapproved (particularly of the boy, who would of course carry on the family name)." It looks from this account as though the inhabitants of a small country village may be more tolerant than those of a large town. But one must beware of drawing conclusions from a single instance as this finding may appertain to the particular village or, even more likely, to the reputation and influence of the Copse parents.

Let us turn now to the letter from Mrs Jennifer Wood. She writes more chattily and warmly than the Copses, but she comes over as equally objective and balanced:

Dear Dr Heim,

Have just received your two letters from my sister-in-law, June Logan. We seem to be very late on the scene! But just a few notes on our adopted daughter.

We have four natural children – at the time of adoption (or rather the arrival of our adoptee) they were ten, eight, seven and five respectively and were consulted on our decision to adopt. Our new daughter was five months old and had been with three different foster mothers. She is half French West African, half American Jewish white – and now aged fourteen years. I cannot honestly say we have had any problems that could be laid at Adoption's door. As a matter of principle, we have used racist epithets as pet names and obviously she has met prejudice – but having met ugly words in love, she has not recognised them in hate, e.g. being greeted at School as "nig-nog" and replying "how did you know my nickname?" She has grown up so like our other children that it is difficult to believe in heredity, except for an amazing sense of rhythm and a gift for mimicry. Any other difference can be explained entirely by having four adoring elder siblings to spoil her.

The only difficult period (difficult only in the sense that it was

94

not as easy as others) was when she first arrived – we had to wait nine months for legal adoption (this being advised procedure at the time in cases of black babies); and as a mother, when she was ghastly and screamed, I knew she wasn't really mine. We have often felt that if we were younger and starting again, we would have "collected" children rather than had four of our own. Our daughter knows as much about her natural parents as we do, but except for a short time aged five, when she would threaten me that she was going back to her first mummy, has not yet expressed any interest in them. She also sees no incongruity in being a black child in a white family.

We used to live, until six months ago, in a small provincial town where everyone knew who she was but, as you can see, now live in the East End. I feared for her with the dramatic change, aged thirteen, and the sudden discovery that twenty-five per cent of Hackney was black too, but the hang-ups were entirely mine!

We feel always that there will be difficulties ahead as she grows up but that these are probably racial, not "adoptive".

There is one thing I should like to have written at the beginning. Our decision to adopt our daughter was instantaneous when we heard her story, but we were made to wait a month, then visit her. Her foster-mother then told me how to look after her and I remember feeling incensed that she should instruct me on how to care for my own daughter. My husband swallowed her whole in the same way. We have probably made hundreds of mistakes according to the textbooks, including changing her name as we couldn't bear the one she had, but honestly don't believe they were different mistakes than we made with our other children.

I don't expect you really wanted any of this sort of information as I have written it – just a long gabble. Adoption has not seemed to pose any problems not already inherent in bringing up children. But if you would like to contact us [telephone number given] please do, if you feel we could be any help. I have shown your other letter to our daughter, but so far no reaction at all!

Yours sincerely,
Jennifer Wood

Here once again is colour-prejudice encountered in school – this time brilliantly met by the use of "racist epithets as pet names" at home. This is a tactic that all adoptive parents with coloured children may do well to note. From the viewpoint of this book, perhaps the most interesting comment is that, "We have often felt that if we were younger and starting again, we would have 'collected' children rather than had four of our own." To express such a sentiment – whether or not the Woods actually would have taken this course, if they had thought of it earlier – indicates their unusual outlook on life. One cannot say here, "Ah, they're rationalising," or "They don't realise what it means to have children born to you," since they have had four children born to them.

These three families have a lot to teach us, not only about coloured adoptees – though their narratives are indeed informative on this score – but also on the power and therapeutic value of a love that is unsentimental, generous and realistic.

VII
Drawn Threads

The poor girl had had to suffer the agony of every only child since time began – that is, a crushing and unrelenting canopy of parental worry. Since birth her slightest cough would bring doctors; since puberty her slightest whim summoned decorators and dressmakers; and always her slightest frown caused her mama and papa secret hours of self-recrimination. (John Fowles, *The French Lieutenant's Woman*, Jonathan Cape, 1969.)

It is generally thought that the younger the child at the age of adoption, the happier the outcome. This belief is confirmed by many of our narratives. In the majority of the "success stories" (whether told by adoptee or by parent) the infant came to live with his adoptive parents aged a few weeks – or even a few days; and conversely, in many of the sadder stories, the child was already two, three or even four years of age when adopted. In such cases he not unnaturally remembers what was inevitably a somewhat traumatic event and, of course, if it is rendered doubly traumatic by such treatment as witnessing the destruction of a favourite toy or the disposal of familiar garments, the distressing flavour of the experience may remain with him all his life.

Thus, adoptive parents should aim to receive their child as young as possible. And however keenly they may feel that everything he wears, touches and plays with is to come *from them*, they should recognise that this sentiment is a form of self-indulgence rather than a benefit to the child: this particular "weaning process" should be done gradually, if indeed it is to be done at all. In the unlikely event that a toy, say, has to be destroyed for reasons of hygiene, then the destruction should not occur in the presence of the child. Most of us

97

identify our possessions with ourselves to some extent, even in adulthood, and the young child who suddenly finds himself in a totally new environment is likely to feel bewildered and insecure for a time. His reaction may take the immediate form of crying or restlessness or constantly sleeping – or it may take some little while to manifest itself. In any case, the adoptive parents should be prepared for an initially testing time and, if possible, should themselves assume a relaxed attitude, since tension breeds tension.

The reason that some children do not reach their adoptive parents until they are several years old is often because the biological mother is unwilling to give up her rights to her infant. She cannot or will not take on responsibility for the child at first, but she hopes that her circumstances may change, enabling her to do so at a later date. This sometimes results in the child spending its first years in an institution (calling it a Home does not transform it into a home) or in a foster-home or a series of foster-homes.

Since adoption organisations are liable to believe that blood is necessarily thicker than water, their tendency is to allow the biological mother to take – or to continue to postpone taking – the vital decision. I do not think this is in the best interests of the child and, most adoptive parents would agree, nor therefore is it in *their* best interests. I append, at the end of this chapter, excerpts from an article published in *The Times*, 11 June 1981, as an illustration of just how "thin" blood can sometimes be – and how shockingly lacking in judgment, humanity and essential involvement social workers and doctors can be.

A further point on which agreement obtains in adoptive families is the regret of "only children" that they have no brothers or sisters. Almost all adoptees who had no siblings – either biological or, like themselves, adopted – commented sorrowfully on this fact, saying that they felt acutely the lack of youthful companionship at home. And adoptive parents in retrospect expressed contrition, stating that they later realised that it is a mistake to raise a child on his own: that cousins and young friends, even if living nearby, do not quite make up for being a singleton at home. When the adoptive parents combine rearing an only child with treating him/her very strictly and rigidly enforcing a "no visitors" régime (as did the Maples), life may sometimes appear very thorny to the growing child.

There are, of course, biological offspring who are only children – either because their parents so plan their lives or because, despite their desire for further children, these fail to arrive. The biological only child may also express regret at his lack of siblings but he is more likely to accept this lack as a fact of life than the adoptee – who may feel that his parents having once made the decision to adopt a child could well have adopted one or two more. The adopted "onlies" probably feel their "onliness" to a greater extent than do children born to their parents – though, for both, "onliness" is but a short step to loneliness.

It is not solely in childhood that brothers and sisters provide companionship and moral support (even if a good deal of quarrelling occurs. Learning to quarrel and to make up is an important part of maturing). It can be found heart-warming – and occasionally useful – to the sibling in adulthood and in old age. And, of course, without siblings there can be no nieces and nephews, which again means a considerable deprivation for the adoptee when grown-up. For the adoptees who do not marry and have offspring born to them, it is particularly gratifying to find themselves in an avuncular or aunty role. It may be recalled that several contributors volunteered the information that they felt an intense need to produce progeny: only so could the urgent need they experienced for blood relatives be fulfilled.

From my sample (which may or may not be representative) it appears abundantly clear that adoptees are at no disadvantage whatsoever in finding spouses – and, indeed, in making happy marriages. My impression is that among my correspondents the proportion of men and women who get married between twenty and thirty-five years of age – and who give every promise of living happily ever after – is, if anything, greater than that in the non-adopted population. In view of the prejudice against adoptees that confronted them in some quarters – despite the frequently heard assertion that times have changed in this respect and in respect to illegitimacy – this finding is surprising and heartening.

The negative attitude of some grandparents and some so-called friends towards adoptees, encountered by a few contributors, does seem to present a problem, and its solution is far from easy. Tackling it by means of rational argument is unlikely to succeed, since the negativism is basically irrational. A psychological explanation would be that the trouble-makers are not only unimaginative and self-centred, but that they have unconscious feelings of inferiority. It is possible that they feel inferior because they suspect their biological son/daughter of being infertile. Now a mechanism often used by such people is to *disparage others* – as though the only way to give oneself a leg-up is to push someone else down.

This may be the explanation for the callous way in which some grandparents have declined to recognise the adopted child of their son/daughter; and the "friends" who bestow similar treatment on such a child probably have a built-in feeling of inferiority, or perhaps obscure envy, or possibly a touch of sadism. It is a genuinely difficult situation, bound to cause pain to child and adoptive parent alike; and those who have found themselves suffering from it seem to have responded remarkably sensibly and compassionately – ignoring the hurt, as far as possible, at the time and repaying it with kindness in due course, rather than letting the whirligig of time bring in its revenges.

Another problem met with in our narratives is a feeling of rejection by their biological mother, occasionally expressed by some adopted children; and – linked with this, though not identical with it – the question of illegitimacy. When the latter comes up, as it is likely to do when the child begins to realise its meaning and if he has an intimate, frank relationship with his adoptive parents, there are two main ways of dealing with it. One is the line taken by Mrs Lilac when her son, Ralph, enquired point-blank, "Am I illegitimate?" Having anticipated that the question might arise, she replied easily, "Oh yes, I should think so. Most adopted children are, you know – and so are a lot of non-adopted children." This was accepted in thoughtful silence; Ralph appeared unworried and mildly interested; and he did not refer to the matter again, though the Lilac family prides itself, with reason, on having unreserved discussions on any topic that may present itself.

The second line is the one taken by Mrs Holly, who replied, it may be remembered, "I don't know much about those things." I, personally, prefer the course taken by Mrs Lilac. But adoptive parents who feel strongly on this issue and might therefore feel embarrassed and find it hard to reply simply in the affirmative (assuming this was the case: not all adoptees are illegitimate) would perhaps do better to answer along Mrs Holly's lines. In my opinion the important thing is that the child should not get the impression that it is a shameful or guilt-ridden matter, either for himself or his biological mother.

It is harder to deal with the feeling of rejection – if this should arise in the mind of the adoptee. "Why didn't my mother want to keep me?" is a question that occurs several times in the narratives. Here again I favour a cool, factual response: perhaps, "It would have been very difficult for her – she was all alone, you see," or, "Well, she didn't have much money – and she couldn't have kept both you and her

100

job" – the answer given being the closest to the circumstances of the child's biological mother at that time. But whatever the answer, it is reassuring if followed up spontaneously with some such remark as, "Thank goodness she couldn't keep you, or *we* might never have got you!"

This brings me to two further threads: should the child be told that (s)he is adopted? And, if so, at what age should this information be imparted? Briefly the answers are, respectively, "Yes, always", and "from the very beginning". My reasons are as follows.

If the child is brought up in the belief that he was born to his adoptive parents, sooner or later he is bound to learn that he was in fact adopted. This discovery seems almost inevitable. Either some officious "well-wisher" volunteers the information, or a relative inadvertently drops a hint, or the adoptee comes across relevant letters or documents. Not only is this revelation an immense and painful shock to him, destroying the very fabric of his home life, but it sows in him a seed of distrust of his adoptive parents. If they have misled him in this, may they not have deceived him in other ways? How can mutual love and communication flourish where deception lies at the root of a relationship? How *could* they do this to him? . . .

These are the kind of emotions that arise; and many an adoptee, on learning the truth in this way, has packed his bag and left home. The older he is when he learns the facts, the more upset he is likely to be. This is why he should be told of his adoptive status at the earliest possible moment and, if he is adopted in infancy, this means long before he can fully understand its meaning. The realisation will then dawn gradually.

The babe-in-arms should always be introduced as "our adopted son" or "our adopted daughter". Thus, when at one or two years of age (s)he begins to understand language, the child is used to hearing this phrase, and is prepared for its elucidation at a later date. The explanation may be an effort for the parent to give, and for the child to take, even at four or five – but it is very much harder on both sides if the adoptee is as old as ten, let alone fourteen or fifteen. The child should learn the facts *very young* and *from the adoptive parents themselves*.

The truth, and nothing but the truth, is the best policy in this vital matter, as indeed it is in all issues concerning parent/child. Quite apart from any questions of principle or of ethics, it is the wisest strategy since consistency is almost impossible in the absence of honesty, and the truth has a disconcerting habit of asserting itself when thought to have been comfortably suppressed.

My insistence on telling the child, and giving the information right from the start, is in accordance with official adoption practice. But after this our paths diverge, in two respects. It seems to me that the fact of adoption should be readily and openly acknowledged – not just to the immediate family and a few close friends. For if the adoptee becomes aware of any secrecy or reserve on the matter, he is liable to infer that there is something nasty in that particular woodshed. If not, why conceal the fact? Children do tend to be very logical until they gradually become contaminated by the special pleading and double standards of most adults.

This is related to the extreme care taken by Adoption Organisations, and mentioned several times in the narratives, to find children who physically resemble their future adoptive parents, in hair- and eye-colour, body-build and facial features. This suggests a desire on the part of the organisations to play down the fact of adoption – as well as, of course, to enable the adoptive parents to identify as deeply and as quickly as possible with their child.

It seems to me far less important to match for physical features than for psychological qualities, such as sense and sensibility. As suggested above, there is nothing remotely furtive or pitiable about adoption, and it is vital that all concerned should recognise this fact and act in accordance with it. Many children born to their parents are markedly different from them in appearance (sometimes, also, in intellect and emotions). Moreover, as vividly described by Geoff Ebony (pp. 32–33) one *becomes like* people one lives with – particularly if there is mutual liking and respect. As Ebony writes: " . . . mannerisms of speech and movement, even modes of thinking, are just as powerful recognition-signals as physical resemblance". He goes on to say that he "had absorbed a great many of [his] father's behavioural character-istics". Incidentally, this is largely the basis of the opinion often voiced that married couples resemble each other in appearance. The similarity, where it exists, resides in their gestures, intonations and expressions (verbal and facial) rather than in their physical features.

It is my belief, therefore, that physical resemblance between adoptive parent and child is relatively unimportant. And, as more and more parents are adopting infants from the other ends of the earth, this is evidently a belief that is on the increase.

A further point on which I differ from officialdom concerns the law making it mandatory to allow adopted offspring to trace their biological parent(s) if they so desire: the 1975 Children's Act, Section 26. This description of the recent Law is something of a simplification.

I have given it in the form that most people believe it to take.

More precisely, the Law states that people adopted after 12 November 1975 are entitled to have access to the original birth-records and to counselling by a social worker. They would thus approach the Local Authority. For those adopted before 1975, it is *compulsory* to receive counselling from a social worker, if the original birth certificate is sought! In either case, a good deal of research may be required. I believe – after having devoted much time and thought to the question – that this Law was ill-conceived. I did not at first hold this view, realising that it was drafted by well-meaning people with the interests of the adoptee in mind, but I now believe them to have been mistaken. (I am not personally involved on this issue, as neither my son nor my daughter have ever evinced the slightest desire to contact their biological parents.)

On exploring the matter, I gain the impression that seeking out the biological mother may prove disruptive both to her and her offspring (past or present). The views expressed by Audrey Medlar, Jane Hawthorn, Mary Fir and Keith Rosewood are relevant here. It tends, moreover, to be the less settled adoptees who contemplate taking advantage of this recently passed Law. Since its repeal, at least in the near future, is unlikely, the setting-up of the various hurdles seems to be highly desirable.

When one considers the several recipients of my circular letter who feared to stir up waters described by them as untroubled – when they were merely asked to write down their views, in confidence – one begins to realise how deeply disturbing the seeking and the eventual meeting might prove to adoptee, adoptive parent and biological parent – especially perhaps the latter. If the biological mother is in fact upset at having her long-buried past exhumed and presented to her in latter-day guise, her dismay is likely to communicate itself to her biological son/daughter, and this again may brush off on to the adoptive parents. None of these hypotheses takes into account the shock caused to the adoptee by the almost inevitable differences between the two homes, whatever form these may take, and the equally probable conflict of loyalties and resentments aroused, even in cases where the contact is welcomed.

Coda to Chapter VII

The purpose of this coda is to give a practical and well-publicised illustration of the water-thinness of some parents' blood. Indeed – to pursue the metaphor – what runs in the veins of some parents is not so much *water* as virulent poison. I refer to the cases of child-neglect and child-battering that periodically hit the headlines.

In these cases, one or both the miscreants are, I believe, most often the biological parent(s) of the child concerned. It seems to be worth quoting from one of the many instances because of the still widely held belief in the sanctity of the parent/child bond and the over-riding authority of the social worker. Moreover, the case in point is quite recent, reported in *The Times* of 11 June 1981, and the view is sometimes expressed that the bad old days of child-abuse are ended – their badness referring to the time when parents-to-be had often left school in their early teens or younger, when there were no salaried experts whose job it was to protect young children and when the few people who did take an active interest were "amateurs", i.e. neighbours or kind-hearted, commonsensical volunteers who had not received the training that official social workers get nowadays.

The following report is not unique. On reading it, the earlier case of Maria Colwell irresistibly comes to mind, along with the assurances made at the time that measures would be taken to ensure that a child should never again fall through the net owing to misjudgment or failure of communication among the relevant officials.*

Excerpts from an article in *The Times*, 11 June 1981:

Maria Mehmedagi, aged eleven months, died from severe battering ... according to the report of an independent inquiry, published yesterday† ... Two doctors at the hospital where the baby had an operation for a stomach blockage at four weeks, suspected child abuse but did not inform the family doctor, community health or social services. Nor did the hospital inform anyone that her mother failed to keep appointments after the operation.

The family doctor did not pass on his own suspicions and the two hospitals involved did not communicate with each other. Community nurses in two London boroughs failed to communicate with each other when the girl was placed in foster care ... The social worker did not give, nor the probation officer seek,

*Report of the Committee of Inquiry into the Care & Supervision Provided in Relation to Maria Colwell, London, HMSO, 1974.
†*Maria Mehnedagi – Report of an Independent Inquiry*, published by London Borough of Southwark, Lambeth, Southwark & Lewisham Area Health Authority & the Inner London Probation & After-Care Service.

information necessary to provide the court with a proper social inquiry report, and vital information from the foster mother and social work assistants was not passed on. Nor was the evidence available properly emphasized to the case conference that decided to send the baby home.

Finally, the CID did not give the juvenile bureau sufficient information on their involvement or views on the case, which were strongly against her being returned home. The result of these failures was that all the professional workers approached the case from the wrong perspective and assumed she should be returned home without considering other options . . .

The report implies that the child's life might have been even shorter but for the persistence of a health-visitor standing in for a colleague who was on leave. On her own initiative, she visited the family and found the baby bruised on her face, head and shoulder. The health-visitor rang the family doctor, who did not visit, but suggested that the baby be brought to his evening surgery. The health-visitor then rang a senior clinical medical officer, who declined to take action. The health-visitor later got in touch with a partner of the family doctor, who immediately visited the home, and arranged for the baby to be admitted to hospital the same day.

She was admitted to hospital on 17 January 1978 aged seven weeks and found to have a fractured collar bone, irreversible damage to the tissues around her left thigh bone, and bruising to her forehead, right cheek, below her right eye, and around her right knee and thigh. Subsequent examination of X-rays taken showed that she also had three fractured ribs. These injuries were the third sustained by the child, but, because previous suspicions were not communicated, the incident was treated as an isolated one though sufficiently alarming for immediate action to be taken. The baby's father was charged, and subsequently convicted of causing actual bodily harm. He was placed on probation for two years . . .

. . . When the conference reconvened, relevant information about previous suspicions of abuse and feeding difficulties were not considered. Administrative decisions were taken, but the baby's future was not considered. She remained in hospital for nearly six months, while a succession of interim care orders were obtained. She was finally discharged from hospital on 13 June to foster parents who could have taken her in February, which would have been preferable according to the report. A conference on 6 July decided that she should be sent home to her parents.

The first home visit was on 25 July, when the probation officer collected her from the foster-parents and delivered her to her parents . . . The social worker visited that evening and found them "happy, relaxed and being very much a family". Then he went on leave and returned on the day of an official strike. He never saw the child again. Her home visits continued, with social work assistants taking over the job of collecting her from the foster-home and taking her to her parents. Both assistants noticed that Maria had facial scratches and bruising, and the foster mother was also worried about her condition . . .

Despite the danger-signals, a case conference on 11 October decided to continue with the plan to send the baby home full-time, though still on trial and subject to a care order. She went home on 16 October. Nine days later she was found to have lost 11.5 oz in weight in a week, but the health-visitor did not intervene. She was admitted to hospital on 31 October suffering from severe brain damage, a fractured skull, a bite mark and multiple minor bruises. She died four days later. Her father was sentenced to nine months' imprisonment for causing actual bodily harm, but cleared of manslaughter. . .

The director of social services for Southwark said yesterday that the easy way to deal with such cases was not to take risks and keep the child away from the parental home. But he did not believe in playing safe, which might be illegal in any case if that meant taking a child away from home . . . Every week, Southwark receives ten initial referrals on child abuse. There are 392 battered children on the council's child abuse register just now, the Press Association reports.

The excerpts from this report raise several important issues. But I am concerned mainly with the crucial fact that it was Maria's biological father who battered her, and ultimately caused her death. Her natural parents were given priority over foster-parents "who could have taken her" earlier; and it was the *foster*-mother (among others) who was "worried about her condition".

This book deals with adoption rather than fostering, but my impression is that few if any adoptive parents (or foster-parents) achieve the depths of brutality that are sometimes plumbed by biological parents: yet it is the latter to whom officialdom automatically

106

awards priority. The authorities would surely – and correctly – have vetoed the right of an adoptive couple to have back Maria, in the circumstances, however "happy, relaxed and being very much a family", the social worker might have judged them to be. Note the reported comment made by the director of social services for Southwark, "that the *easy* way [my italics] to deal with such cases was not to take risks and keep the child away from the parental home. But he did not believe in playing safe, which might be illegal in any case if that meant taking a child away from home."

This comment strikes the outside observer as tragi-comic in its complacency and sophistry. In the first place "the easy way" is surely the line that was taken, namely, ignoring the danger-signals, failing to communicate among the many who knew how Maria's parents treated her and failing to take action (with the exception of one health-visitor, who did combine courage with persistence). Such negativism can scarcely be described as the hard way.

Secondly, the vaunted taking of risks concerns here the well-being of an eleven-month-old child rather than the well-being of medical and social workers. Incidentally, the implication in the report is repeatedly that it is *death* that is the horror – presumably because it has an objectivity, a finality and a legality that suffering, however intense and prolonged, is evidently thought not to have. Thirdly, those in charge of the social services should really make up their minds whether they prefer to seek refuge in their willingness, and that of their colleagues, to take alleged risks, or in the possibility that removing a child from home "might be illegal". The latter is improbable where home-life involves the fracturing of skull, collar-bone and ribs in addition to being bruised, scratched and bitten.

The earlier, Colwell, case resembles the Mehmedagi case in several respects: the repated physical assaults on the child, the lack of communication among officials and – most to the point – the fact that the child was returned to her biological mother and that the injuries which led to death took place in her house. The main differences between the two tragedies are: (a) that Maria Colwell, when returned to her mother, was six years of age and therefore able to plead, as she persistently did, to be allowed to go back to her foster-parents with whom she had lived happily and securely for most of her life (and to whom she tried to run away on several occasions); (b) that most of the physical injuries seem to have been inflicted by Maria Colwell's step-father – though there is evidence of considerable mental cruelty on the part of her biological mother.

107

As the Colwell Report comments (page 83, para. no. 232): "Regulation 17 of the Regulations of 1955 . . . provides that a child shall not be boarded out unless the foster-parents and their home have been favourably reported on; that their reputation and religious persuasion and their suitability in age, character, temperament and health has likewise been ascertained, and also that no member of the household is suffering from any physical or mental illness which might affect the child . . ." These factors are evidently scarcely considered when a child is being returned to biological parent(s) – whatever the expressed anguish of longstanding foster-parents or of the child.

An experienced and compassionate social worker of my acquaintance points out to me that the greater humanity of adoptive parents is a comparatively recent phenomenon; that the extreme rarity of child-abuse in such homes is due largely to changes in the relevant legislation during the last few decades; and that the absence of child-battering among adoptive parents is a tribute to the improved selection of such parents by social workers. She tells me that the criteria for the choice of parents have shifted from material standards (such as number of bedrooms in the house, income of parents, etc.) to considerations such as the motivation and family feeling of the would-be adopters and the affection they have to bestow. These are, of course, far more difficult to assess than are material factors, and credit should go to the social workers for their relative success in this area.

VIII
Generation Gaps and Links

Biological sons and daughters are apt to take for granted all that their parents do for them. If all has gone well, the younger generation expects that their needs will be provided for as a matter of course; that when they are grown-up, home will continue to be ever-welcoming; and that home includes parents – who may be irritatingly inquisitive or obtrusive at times, but who have their uses, be it as launderers, as hosts for other young people, as warehouse-keepers or, in due course, as baby-sitters for grandchildren.

Parents sometimes complain of being thus taken for granted – forgetting that they behaved very similarly with *their* parents – but in general they accept it, enjoying the feeling of still being needed, of being able to compete conversationally with the Joneses and of having a future to live for as well as a past to live in.

The picture that emerges from the narratives of adoptees, however, is sometimes slightly different. Many of them express *gratitude* to their adoptive parents, *regret* that they have not always behaved as these would have wished, and occasional feelings of *guilt* are mentioned if the adoptee has tried, or even contemplated trying, to trace his biological parents. Geoff Ebony once again puts it well (page 34) when he says that "a sense of obligation is probably the unique province of the adopted child".

Such cases seem to me to be less satisfactory than those in which the adoptee expresses no such sentiments. If he feels grateful, the parents may well have implied at some stage that they were doing him a favour. But a child no more asks to be adopted than a biological child asks to be born. If adoptees compare their home-life with life in an institution, this comparison has in all probability been suggested to

109

them: such a suggestion should never be made. The adoptive parents should be clear in their own minds that they wanted to adopt because they wanted children: in this regard, it was an egocentric – not an altruistic – thing to do. There is nothing "wonderful" or self-denying about it!

The judgment of adoption officers is not infallible: if it were, they would be unique. But there are at least two criteria which they would do well to bear in mind when selecting parents for the dwindling number of babies who are available for adoption. If they have reason to suppose that one or both members of the couple see themselves as philanthropic; if there is any discernible element of smugness ("it seems the least we can do – we have so much to offer"), or of good works ("poor fatherless infant"), or of looking for returns ("after all, we're not so young now – who's going to look after *us* in our old age?"), these seem to me to be contra-indications of adoptive suitability. And they are surely the ones who say in due course – or who imply it – "after *all* we have done for you . . . how *could* you . . .", or "how can you *not* . . ." This attitude is sometimes found also in biological parents where it is, of course, equally deplorable, but I think it affects their younger generation less poignantly.

A second contra-indication is seen in the couple who decide to adopt in the hope that the infant will shore up the marriage. The child should be considered an end in himself, not a means to an ulterior end. If the marriage shows any signs of disintegrating, the adoption of a child is just as likely to break the camel's back as to nourish it! I would go further: in my opinion adoptees should be granted only to couples who have a close, stable, enduring relationship and both of whom strongly desire children. I know of several cases where the parents have split up after they have adopted, and this can have a shattering effect on the child. Let me give two examples, drawn from real life.

The Junipers, after some years of childless marriage, decided to adopt and they acquired a healthy, pretty little girl, Louise, aged a few weeks. All went well until some four years later when – Mr Juniper and another (married) woman becoming strongly attracted to each other – he and Mrs Juniper felt that the only course open to them was to separate. They continue to inhabit the same small provincial town. Louise lives with her mother but she sees her father regularly once or twice a week. From having been a cheerful, active, companionable but self-contained child, Louise has become anxious, tense, querulous and constantly demanding attention by non-stop talking. Since the parents – especially the father – feel at fault, they try to compensate by spoiling her, both materially and emotionally. A vicious spiral has been set up.

My second example concerns the Hazels, who had adopted Simon, an attractive, highly intelligent, sensitive baby boy. Again all had gone well until Simon reached the age of three. In this case it was Mrs Hazel who defected, claiming that her husband, a scientist at a Northern university, was not devoting enough time to her and Simon ("he only plays with him in the evenings and at weekends"), and finding also that she was in love with a young man, some fifteen years her junior. She wished to marry him and to keep the boy. The father also wished to keep his son, so that Simon found himself, at under four years of age, the fraying rope in a tug-of-war.

No doubt both these couples had appeared happily and stably married when they applied to their adoption organisation. Otherwise they would probably not have been accepted as adoptive parents. But there must have been some indication of immaturity on the part of at least one member of each pair – or so hindsight would lead one to expect.

The outcome in these two cases is not yet known, Louise and Simon still being children. But there is little doubt that both have been submitted to a severe, long-lasting emotional strain or that both will remain only children, without the benefit of siblings with whom to share sorrows – and joys. This lack is still more important in one-parent than in two-parent families. The stress of parent-separation is often inflicted nowadays on biological offspring since married couples seem to split up almost as frequently as they remain united. When it happens to the parents of adoptees, however, its repercussions are apt to be even more serious for the child than is the case in biological families. This is partly because, as we have already seen, the adopted child tends to be somewhat more vulnerable; and partly because in biological families the split-up often occurs after several children have been born, in which event the offspring do at least have the consolation of intimately knowing – and perhaps living with – other children in the same boat.

The father/mother separation does not always result in a one-parent family. On the contrary, the child sometimes finds himself in the rather bewildering position of having two fathers and two mothers – if not more! This sometimes works out well and sometimes not so well, but it is a problem which is outside the scope of this book. The question of one-parent families *is* within its scope, however, for the powers-that-be in their habitually fashion-changing way are beginning to extol the virtues of allowing a single woman to adopt a child* – as opposed to their avowed, rigid practice some years ago. The pros and cons of the one-parent family are discussed in the next chapter.

Before we leave the issue of generation gap, however, we should discuss the question of the age of the parents at the time of adoption. This is evidently considered crucial by the authorities since in some countries the adoption organisations will not contemplate granting a child to parents who are over forty years of age whereas, in other countries, the *minimum* age deemed acceptable is forty! Whilst this evinces a certain element of arbitrariness, it shows too that the question demands serious thought.

The motives inspiring these two conflicting regulations are fairly obvious. If the would-be mother is under forty she may yet produce children – and, however ardently one may support the principle of adoption, it has to be admitted that most parents, given the possibility, would prefer to have offspring born to them. As Sylvia Rowan puts it (Chapter II), " . . . in some way pregnancy and childbirth are a crucial part of the parent/child bond . . . when the child is wanted, a new-born baby is the product of a love and is like a combination of the two people who created it . . ."

On the other hand, if the adoptive parents are over forty they are likely to be less in touch with the younger generation, both mentally and physically; they may find it harder to cope with the demands of the young child and – very different but equally exhausting – the demands of the teenager; and their children may find them more set in their ways than the parents of their friends.

Like most generalisations there is some truth in these arguments but they fail, inevitably, to take account of individual differences. Twenty-five years ago I found the powers-that-be were rather rigid on the question of age-of-adopter: they considered only the under-forties (and, at that time they affirmed, understandably, that "it is important for a baby to have the security and affection of two parents"). However, the Matron through whom I eventually acquired my second adoptee – and to whom I had confided, with trepidation, that I was then forty-three years old – wrote, "I think that the real deciding factor in adoption is the maturity of the adopter."

Naturally I liked this attitude! But she and I would have agreed that

---

*See, for example, Sharen Aoki, "Single-parent adoption", and Maggie Cook, "Single-parent adoption: a British case", both in *Adoption & Fostering*, 89, No. 3 of 1977.

increasing age is no guarantee of increasing maturity: some twenty-year-olds prove impressively mature when given the opportunity to demonstrate this and some people remain surprisingly childish throughout their lives. Maturity in parents is an asset to their children, whether biological or adopted, and no doubt to themselves. The kinds of qualities connoted by the word include tolerance, flexibility and sense of proportion. But it is unfortunately just as difficult to assess these traits in interviews as it is to assess stability – of an individual or of a marriage. As we have seen, this is a difficulty of a very high order.

IX
One-parent Adoptive Families

As the divorce-rate and separation-rate rise, so naturally do the numbers of one-parent families. Clubs and "community centres" are founded – but they scarcely take the place of a reasonably happy marriage, from the viewpoint of either single parent or offspring. School teachers comment lugubriously upon the phenomenon, often attributing to it their increasing anxieties about vandalism, truancy, ungraciousness and failure to take homework seriously. It is likely that some of these problems do stem from lack of a second parent, particularly as more mothers go out to work. When the separated mother gets home – which may be after the child's return from school – she may well feel tired, dispirited and less interested in her child's doings than if she were employed solely in domestic work during the day and expecting the companionship, stimulation and support of her husband later in the evening. (I do realise that not all spouses are companionable, stimulating and supportive but they are more likely to appear so, in their absence!)

This picture, however, is that of the once-married parents who have split up, rather than the deliberately adoptive one-parent family. As we have seen, the latter do exist and it is primarily with them that this chapter deals. The single woman who succeeds in adopting, usually against heavy odds, will probably need to work for financial reasons, but in general she will not feel lonely, unstimulated or unsupported when she rejoins her child(ren) in the evening. For her the comparison is between having *their* company or, herself, returning to an empty house. She is therefore greatly appreciative of their presence and she is unlikely either to take the children for granted or to regard them as burdensome.

114

Since we are concerned here with the one-parent household, we shall concentrate primarily on the adoptive mother who is unmarried. As already suggested, she will find much joy in her children for she will have expended a great deal of time and energy in obtaining them. Quite apart from the fact that it is a common human trait to treasure what has been hard to attain, unless she had had an exceptionally strong maternal instinct she would probably not have embarked on the countless formalities and the almost endless periods of waiting.

As Tony Pine picturesquely put it (page 9): "A strong point I have always felt in favour of being an adopted child is that you know definitely that you were wanted very badly by your adoptive parents. Otherwise they would not have gone through all the rigmarole to get me. Or at least, I would never think that my adoptive parents had got me by accident (though my natural ones very probably did!)"

Biological parents will often say, casually, about one of their offspring, "Well, he wasn't *planned*, but we find we're really very fond of him, now he's here." They are quite liable to say this to an adoptive parent, evidently unaware of the heartache that accompanies, first, longstanding childlessness; then the suspense of the probation-period, during which the biological mother may change her mind; then, the long haul involved in acquiring an adoptee; and, finally, the inexpressible joy of having eventually got there. This joy is a long-term asset to the adoptee.

It is clear from what is said in Chapter VIII that the unmarried one-parent adoptive family is a very different proposition from the adoptive family whose parents have split up. Whilst it is true that in the latter case, the child will have had the benefit of a "normal background" at first – in the sense of having both a mother and a father – he will probably have suffered for some time from discord between his parents and, later, from their separation. Neither of these stresses arise when the adoptive mother is unmarried.

There is no opportunity for adult bickering in her household. From the time the adoptee arrives in her home, the single mother has the first and last word – until the child reaches the articulate stage! If a nanny or an *au pair* girl is employed, he will still know that Mum is the vital one, that Mum takes the decisions, and he will not be torn asunder by disputes or quarrels between his parents. On the other hand, he will be well-acquainted with several other adults from an early stage and, as I suggest in the second part of the book, this is highly desirable.

It is even more important for the single adoptive parent than it is for parents living together to adopt more than one child. A one-to-one relationship between the generations may be very heart-warming and fulfilling for both parties, but if it is too exclusive and long-lasting it may have dangers. It may result in mutual over-protectiveness, in an inability to form close relationships with others and – if either side does eventually form an attachment of any kind elsewhere – in painful jealousy. At least two infants, therefore, should be adopted. Furthermore, the single parent should take her children to visit, and to stay with, a variety of friends and relatives; and she should frequently invite to the house men and women friends of all ages.

When her children make friends of their own, these too should be made welcome at home. She should gladly accept invitations on her children's behalf – and, when they are old enough to go on their own, she should not insist on accompanying them. She should *never* express regret or indignation when she finds her children well able to dispense temporarily with her care and her company. This may seem obvious but it is a mistake made by some parents.

From her own point of view there are certain stresses facing the single-parent adopter. She has no one close and available with whom to discuss childish day-to-day problems – or with whom to share childish day-to-day triumphs. If she does "use" her friends in this way, she is liable to discover that most people have a low threshold of boredom where the success and failure of other people's children are concerned. Indeed, if she persists she may even find this a potent recipe for turning friends into distant acquaintances!

A further lack is a second authority, who might be expected to back her up when, as happens from time to time, she has trouble with the children. It would be particularly useful when the children are teenagers to be able to say, sometimes, "Well, you know what I think. Let's see what your Dad thinks about it, when he gets home." Even if Dad is going to disagree with Mum or, maybe, produce yet a third point of view, the discussion gains a new dimension; the matter is better aired with two interested adults rather than one; the child's resentment may be divided between two people or may alternate, instead of being always centred on the one.

Such considerations are bound to arise in most single adoptive households. Finally, there is the inevitable question of dreariness when the birds have flown. "Let the children go" is good advice if one wishes "to keep" them, in any sense. But the house is sadly quiet without them, and, although in theory one may look forward to receiving mail, the present generation of young people is not keen on letter-writing. What assemblage of parents, adoptive or otherwise, has not said this? The feeling of loss applies equally, of course, to widows and widowers whose biological children have grown up and left home. It is the other side of the happiness-coin.

Where other people's families are concerned it is all too easy to point out that now is the time for the mother to pursue all the interests for which she previously could not find the time, and that the "children" must achieve full independence for their own good and that this can be done only by leaving home. The latter sentiment is surely correct but it looks somehow less convincing when one is the parent concerned and has no spouse with whom to share the initial loneliness. As to the pursuit of interests: this demands an energy that tends to decrease with advancing years and – interesting in its own right – that diminishes proportionately as *joie de vivre* diminishes.

However, if all has gone well, the birds – having been encouraged to spread their wings – may indeed return to the nest occasionally. In due course, they may even bring with them a fledgling or two, inducing a pleasurable, albeit illusory, sense of immortality.

X
Conclusion

Part I of this book is intended to be a qualitative survey of adoption from the viewpoints of both the adoptee and the parent. I have eschewed statistics and have made no attempt to produce quantitative evaluations of any kind. My aim has been to *get the feel* of adoption – aware that the relevant laws and customs are in constant flux and that the feeling will be to some extent peculiar to each individual and each family.

I have therefore relied very heavily on my contributors and, rather less heavily, on my own experience. I have taken the information supplied by my correspondents at its face value, that is, I assume that the majority have told me the fundamentals as perceived by them. They will have been, of course, highly selective: otherwise each contribution would have been endless. But apart from this purely practical issue, in some cases they will probably have deliberately omitted points that are too painful or intimate to bear the light of day, and they will inevitably have forgotten or repressed certain others.

Despite these caveats I am inclined to believe that between us, my contributors and I have got to the guts of the matter. This hopeful belief is based on four grounds: (a) the fact that my contributors were self-selected – in that those who did not wish to reply ignored my circular letter or wrote explaining their reasons for not co-operating; (b) the fact that a fair proportion of both adoptees and parents did admit discontents and regrets, and specified the causes, often in great detail; (c) the open-ended form of my letters resulted in correspondents having to decide for themselves which aspects of adoption were the most significant; (d) despite the variety in age and circumstances obtaining among contributors, they showed a considerable measure of agreement about what are the most important factors in adoption. Let us discuss these four points in turn.

(a) It may seem strange that I should put the self-selection of contributors on the credit side, especially in view of the already highly selective nature of my original sample. My reason for so doing is that it implies that those who participated did so willingly and co-operatively; that they were actively interested and thought the project worthwhile. This optimism is confirmed by their giving their name, address and telephone number in all but two cases (despite my assurance that this was unnecessary) and their frequently offering to supply further information and to receive a visit from me.

My hopefulness that the self-selection did not increase the unrepresentativeness of the sample was upheld by point (b) – the dissatisfaction and resentment expressed by some correspondents and the "failure" admitted by some adoptive parents. It is well known that usually less than fifty per cent of people will respond positively when requested to take part in any sort of social survey. Some are apathetic, some mean to reply but "forget" or indeed forget, some do not wish "to get involved" and some are professional non-co-operators, righteously indignant at what they see as yet another invasion of privacy or impertinent claim on their time. To these normal reactions must be added the vulnerability of the adoptive parents and their child. It may be recalled, incidentally, that I never approached adoptees under sixteen years of age. This was partly because, conscious of the sensitivity of the whole area, I was particularly anxious not to disturb anyone very young, and partly because fewer than sixteen years of adoption seemed to me too short a period to enable valid conclusions to be reached.

While naturally saddened by the narratives that expressed disappointment or anger or sorrow, I was in a sense glad to receive these replies since they were usually instructive and they suggested that the self-selectiveness of my sample did not go all one way.

It may be remembered that a few correspondents objected to my not having used the more conventional approach of the questionnaire. Some described my circular letter as rather vague and others said that it would have been easier to respond had it consisted of a list of questions. The latter were surely quite right: it is far easier to answer (probably monosyllabically) a series of questions, devised by someone else, than it is to think up for oneself the vital issues and to write articulately about them. However, those adoptees and adoptive parents who succeeded in cogitating and formulating their thoughts

119

did, for the most part, produce enlightening material and – point (d) – where the chosen topics of contributors overlapped, a good measure of agreement was found. The justification for the open-ended method, however, lies in the *variety* of topics chosen and of attitudes to these topics. The questionnaire technique does not permit of such an outcome. It assumes that the investigator knows in advance what are the crucial issues and that the respondents will be able to reply in a uniform, and usually a simple, way.

What, then, are the objections to the open-ended circular letter, from the viewpoint of the research worker who wishes to make a qualitative study? For this particular project, the main objection is perhaps that the technique may increase the self-selectivity of the participants. It would be unlikely to attract people who doubt their ability to express themselves on paper and who are unused to doing so. It is true that my sample of contributors tended to be better educated, more intelligent and to have more "social conscience" than would a cross section of the population. But I gather that the population of adoptive parents generally *is* above average in education, intelligence and social awareness. This may be partly for economic reasons – children being fairly expensive luxuries, and financial success being correlated with education and intelligence (although there are clearly many exceptions to this generalisation).

The social conscience question is particularly interesting for I gained the impression, as I read and re-read the replies to my two circular letters, that not only do adoptive *parents* tend to go in for work of a "caring" kind, either paid or voluntary, but that a disproportionately high fraction of *adoptees* do likewise. Whether the latter phenomenon is due primarily to environment or heredity would not be easy to establish – if we wished to do so.

This point leads on to the question of the original background of the adopted child. How much of it is known to the adoption organisations? And how much of their knowledge do they pass on to the adoptive parents? In my own case I was informed of the ages, nationalities and occupations of the two relevant couples, and also of the occupations of one set of grandparents (all of which I passed on to my daughter and son as soon as they were old enough to understand). I believe this sort of information, plus facts about any marked aptitudes, such as art, and constitutional strengths or weaknesses, such as athletics, asthma – when known – are nowadays conveyed to the adoptive parents. There are cases, of course, where little or nothing is known on the father's side.

I have heard it suggested when, for instance, the adopted child of a musician grows up to become a composer or a pianist, say, that this is an example of the "self-fulfilling prophecy": that the adoptive parents knowing of the child's musical background have fostered this and inevitably produced a musician. But this seems to be an over-statement. There is undoubtedly a genetic element in many mental gifts and many traits of temperament; the influence of environment is also strong: the interaction of the two is all-important. And just as there is said to be "assortative mating" (like tending sometimes to marry like) so attempts are made to match available infants to adoptive parents – with varying degrees of success as has been seen.

We have come full circle and we are now perhaps in a better position to answer the question, Thicker Than Water? Is it true that blood is thicker than water? The question, in effect, is asking whether blood relatives *feel* closer and *act* closer to one another, than people do who are unrelated by ties of blood. And, further, is the felt-closeness correlated with the degree of closeness of the relationship?

Were it not for my aversion to the simple affirmative/negative where complex human questions are concerned, I would reply unreservedly NO! Tales such as that told at the end of Chapter VII indicate all too strongly how water-thin the blood-tie of parent/infant can be. Whilst tales such as those told by the Rosewoods and the Forests indicate with equal strength how blood-thick the non-sanguineous ties of parent/child sometimes are.

If it shows nothing else, however, Part I of this book shows how rash it is to generalise on this theme, how indefensible to claim that the biological – or, indeed, that the adoptive – parent/child relationship is "the better". Both can be frustrating and agonising, and both can be wonderfully fulfilling.

PART TWO

XI
No Single Best Way

It is one thing to collate the views of adoptees and adoptive parents and to draw conclusions from their experiences, but it is quite another to advise on the upbringing of children generally. Such an undertaking may suggest a certain self-satisfaction on the part of the author: innumerable books on the subject have already appeared. If this one covers the same ground, is it worth writing? And if it disagrees, does this not imply a wilful negativism and smugness in the writer?

I should like to plead that this is not necessarily so, for the following reasons. First, the existing books by no means all accord with one another. There are fashions in child-rearing just as there are fashions in medicine, architecture and clothing. But whilst everyone would agree that the changes in dress are arbitrary and largely dictated by the couturiers – whose aims are predominantly financial – attempts are usually made by doctors and architects to persuade us that the current fashions are an improvement on the old ones. Indeed for many people, in many fields, *newer* means *better* – regardless of the fact that fashions tend to go in cycles.

Secondly, many books on child-rearing present rather extreme views. Some say, "Never pick up a baby when it cries," and, "Don't allow the older child access to its mother for a fortnight after the arrival of a younger sibling."* At the other extreme, it is said that the parent should not punish or even admonish the child, implying that such treatment will harm the child/parent relationship and will arouse feelings of guilt in the child which may have a permanently

---

*Stuart Sutherland, *Breakdown*, p. 10., Paladin Granada, 1977

damaging effect. Part II of this book is intended to offer a middle way, clearly departing from both extremes. (No doubt, those holding the "tough" view will claim that my counsel will result in a "spoilt" child; and adherents of the permissive school will maintain that I understand nothing of the dynamics of childhood.)

Thirdly, I have brought up an adopted daughter and an adopted son from the age of a few weeks, and they are now enjoying life in their mid-twenties. This experience is not, of course, unique, but it is somewhat unusual in that I am a psychologist and unmarried; that I had developed certain ideas about child-rearing in the course of my forty-three years of childlessness; and I did put these ideas into practice when – after a three-year period of refusals and delays – I was eventually allowed to adopt a seven-week-old baby.

Fourthly, and perhaps most important, I do not believe that there is any one best way of bringing up children. I record in this book the methods I used with my two markedly different children, and my grounds for thinking that these methods worked quite well. But I have been struck repeatedly by the remarkable resilience and adaptability of most babies and young children. Those with lazy or selfish parents often appear to survive neglect, harshness and lack of stimulation; whilst the offspring of caring, conscientious parents adapt equally impressively to the current modes of diet, over- or under-protectiveness and psychological fads – whatever they may be!

I have formed the impression over the decades that the one absolute essential for all infants and children is sustained love and affection from at least two people – preferably more – one or another of whom is nearly always around. This love and affection can take many different forms but the young child is generally aware of its existence, even when it takes a somewhat bizarre form (such as is depicted, for instance, in Edmund Gosse's *Father and Son*). In the sad cases where it is lacking, the child usually reacts to this long before he can put the experience into words.

If the parents do not feel warmly towards the infant born to them – and a small minority do not – they should actively consider having the child adopted. To hold on to their baby simply because they feel that society would frown on any other course is unjust to would-be adopters and is probably not in the child's best interests. I know of no evidence to support the widely held doctrine that the "natural" mother is, by virtue of her biological link, the best person to bring up her child. There is, on the contrary, a dismaying amount of evidence of parents battering (occasionally to death) infants born to them (see pages 103–108). Yet moral pressure is often put on the "natural" mother to keep her infant – resulting sometimes in hardship for her and in an insecure environment for the child.

All adoptive parents, on the other hand, intensely want children and they will certainly have a wealth of love and affection to bestow on them. The question is, how to express these feelings. That is basically what the rest of this book is about: my ideas on bringing up offspring, whether these be born to the parents, or adopted, or fostered. The need for love and affection is, I think, common to all children. It is seen as factual and non-controversial. The best *means of expressing* these sentiments, however, is highly debatable.

As is clear from the heading of this chapter, I do not hold that there is one essential best means and that all others should be excluded. Every child is an individual in his own right, as is every parent. Hence there is a sense in which every child/parent relationship – and this is what concerns us – is necessarily unique. But there is also a sense in which members of the family find it unfair if they do not all receive the same treatment from their elders!

The topic abounds in paradoxes of this kind. That and its great social importance renders it absorbing and challenging. Sitting on the fence may be tempting but it is not always very helpful. In the pages that follow, therefore, I endeavour to select a definite point of view and to offer guidelines rather than inflexible rules. The approach is autobiographical to begin with but generalisations come later, complementing my own experience with that of others.

XII
Early Days

Until my long tussle with Officialdom was over, I did not confide to anyone my intention of adopting two babies, one of each sex. And how right I was! When a married couple announce that they are expecting a child, they receive congratulations and good wishes. But in 1955, when success was at last in sight, I received warnings from friends and veiled threats from neighbours. Typical comments were: "You'll never be able to manage to look after a baby and keep up with your work. You've no idea how demanding a young child is"; "I suppose you realise that everybody will assume that they're your own illegitimate infants?"; "You're rather old to start managing a family now – you're over forty, aren't you?"; "You're not going to have *a boy* as well as a girl, surely! He'll be bound to grow up a sissy, with no father-figure to emulate" . . . And the first remark made by my neighbours, with whom I had been (and was later to be) on excellent terms, was, "Well, I hope she won't scream all night."

I realise in retrospect that many of these comments were jocular and probably not unkindly meant. But one is in a vulnerable, hyper-sensitive state when about to embark on the enterprise dearest to one's heart – only too conscious that one might fail, that the biological mother may change her mind and that the authorities may decide, at any time until after the court case, that one is not a fit person to undertake adoptive parenthood.

Once I had acquired my seven-week-old daughter and my carefully selected Yorkshire Nanny, however, things were very different. I then received plenty of help and moral support from friends and, indeed, I have continued to do so over the years. The Nannies (and, later, Mother's Helps) came and went with disconcerting frequency – some left owing to marriage, some owing to pregnancy and some owing to both! But most friends, fortunately, last a lifetime.

In the event, my children did not "scream all night" – or even whimper much during the day. More than once, people said to me, "Why don't your children ever cry?" I told them what I thought was the reason, but they thought it was mostly the luck of the draw. If you do adopt, you must be prepared for the assumption that success of any kind with your children is due to good luck and fortunate heredity. Failures, on the other hand, are due to you and your mode of upbringing! I do not think this form of judgment is made quite as frequently – or, at least, not made so explicitly – with parents rearing children born to them.

This book is not intended to be an autobiographical study of the last twenty-six years of my life, nor as life-histories of my two children. A great deal of what I say is related to them and has been learned from them. Indeed, I have learned from them at least as much as they have learned from me. I shall, however, also be utilising a lot of material based on the children and grandchildren of friends and relatives; and based too on children about whom I have been consulted in my capacity as psychologist.

On the question of gender and of personal pronouns, I propose to use the following convention. I select a name – in this case, Jo – that can apply equally to members of both sexes (short for Joanna or Josephine, Jonathan or Joseph) and shall use the pronouns "she" and "he" for alternate chapters. When I use other names, they will refer to actual children but the name itself will always be a pseudonym.

With a child a few weeks old, you are immediately confronted with the basics of life: intake (feeding), output (excretion), sleep and demonstrations of affection. Hunger and thirst are not yet differentiated at this stage; and overt sexual behaviour also takes a little longer to manifest itself. So the next chapters are concerned with the management of feeding, of excreting, of sleeping; and with the joy of caressing and dandling the baby. True, Jo will do the first three instinctively and thus pretty efficiently from the start. But she depends on you to decide *when* she will be offered milk and at what temperature; when she will learn the feel and the look of a chamber-pot; whether she will sleep uninterruptedly through a dark night despite various noises or whether she is to be habituated to absolute silence when in her cot, and to a night-light. She is also dependent on you for her discovery of the delight of body-contact, the mutual warmth and comfort of a cuddle and of a friendly voice and smile.

"A friendly *voice*": the need for this is indeed a basic for the infant and it is not always recognised as such by parents. Jo must be talked to from the very beginning. Some parents do so instinctively and some say little or nothing to their child during the first few weeks or even months. "But an infant a few days old can't understand what you say to it," they reply if taken to task. "Nor could a child of ten – or an adult of twenty – if she had never heard speech," is the answer. The *potential* for language is clearly innate, but this cannot be realised unless the child hears the spoken word.

This fact is fairly obvious if one pauses to think. But it can also be practically observed in several ways. First, the babbling of a baby – and this starts very early – is unmistakably *babbling in a specific language*. An English infant of three months is not actually saying anything, but the noises she emits sound different from the noises emitted, for instance, by a babbling French infant. Even in babyhood the intonation is audibly different – and intonation is an important facet of spoken language, as we all learn when we try to master a foreign tongue. Secondly, a baby intimates remarkably early that she has understood something of the meaning of what is said to her. Her recognition-vocabulary is always far ahead of her spoken vocabulary.

So do talk to Jo from the beginning – while you are feeding her, walking her, changing her nappy, bathing her, dandling her. In the early stages, what you choose to say to her does not terribly matter. She will soon learn to listen and will soon know the difference between a cheerful remark and a sad or angry one – learning to interpret both tone of voice and words used.

Some parents have an irresistible urge to use baby-talk when speaking to infants or young children: "Wozzit diddums, den?" they croon tenderly; and later on, "Where's the choo-choo?", or, "See the moo-moo!" The other day a two-three-year-old walked into a café with her mother and, seeing my dog Marcus seated sedately beside me, she pointed at him, exclaiming in loud delight, "Oh, quack-quack!" (Everyone laughed except Marcus.)

I do not consider that baby-talk actually harms babies or young children, but it seems to me hard that they should have to learn two languages. "Wozzit diddums" is probably untranslatable; but no sooner will Jo have learned the meaning of "choo-choo" than she will have to relearn it as "train". And whilst I am all in favour of teaching Jo the sounds made by various animals – these can be great fun – I think she should grow up with the idea that a *cow* goes "moo" and a *duck* goes "quack-quack".

130

Talking baby-language to Jo suggests to me that she is almost regarded as a member of a different species: in a sense it indicates a lack of respect. Those who indulge in it are liable also to call the child "Baby" for the first year or two, instead of saying "Joanna" or "Jonathan" or whatever the given name may be. This again seems to me a pity, suggesting, as it does, that at this stage the child has no identity or individuality. "Baby" could, after all, be *any* baby, and you will wish Jo from infancy to be well aware of her own identity.

Acquiring the habit of talking to Jo from the start, therefore, is essential. In this way she becomes socialised, she comes to recognise herself and she learns the art of two-way verbal communication. The avoidance of using baby-talk is less crucial but, as I have suggested, it is desirable, to my mind. If you do want Jo to learn two languages while she is young, a second *adult* language should be used – for which Jo may well be grateful for the rest of her life.

XIII
Feeding

Breast-feeding is, alas, usually out of the question for adoptive mothers, but I outline its many advantages and few drawbacks for the benefit of those who do have the choice. Unlike some people, I do not regard this as a moral or ethical issue. Even if the mother is fully equipped, it is surely not her *duty* to breast-feed her baby if she prefers not to do so, since the infants brought up on a bottle are apt to thrive just as well mentally and physically as those who are breast-fed.

Thus I regard it as a matter of personal choice but, for reasons given below, some do consider breast-feeding to be a duty where it is possible. I have discussed the matter with men and women, medically qualified and lay, and interestingly enough I find that those who maintain that biological mothers who choose to bottle-feed their infants are shirking their duty, tend to be male! That breast-feeding confers some benefits, however, is undeniable. The milk is probably ideal for the baby, so no exploring for the right food will be necessary. Whilst a precise estimate of the intake cannot be made, it is virtually impossible to overfeed a breast-fed baby. He may need to be fed more often than infants who are bottle-fed, but – until mixed feeding is begun – neither high nor low frequency of bowel movements need cause anxiety. Both are within the bounds of normality in the breast-fed infant. The milk is "on tap" when required, at just the right temperature and guaranteed untainted (unless, like the wife of Ibsen's Master Builder, the mother succumbs to some arcane fever). It involves an intimate embrace between mother and child but this can be achieved, almost as well, by a reasonably demonstrative and sensuous mother – and not, of course, only during feeding.

Medical evidence supports the view that breast-feeding confers immunity against certain diseases and that breast-fed babies are less liable to diarrhoea and colic than are bottle-fed babies. Some authorities believe that breast-feeding protects against over-sensitivity to proteins, manifested in eczema and other allergic complaints.

It is not the case that breast-feeding deforms the breasts or causes them to sag. I have seen women with exquisite figures, who have breast-fed several children. I am told by a number of mothers who breast-fed their babies that it is a deeply satisfying mental and physical experience – and this I find wholly convincing.

The only drawback, if all goes smoothly, is that the mother must be available whenever Jo is to be fed as this is a function which, in the circumstances, cannot be delegated. Hence if, having elected to breast-feed, she puts Jo's interests first, her freedom will be somewhat curtailed; if, on the other hand, she tends to put her own interests first, Jo's meals may be somewhat delayed or irregular and he is likely to be weaned rather young.

I shall not discuss the relative merits of the various proprietory brands of powdered and tinned milk for babies. Most infants will thrive on any one of these but, if your baby appears to dislike what you offer and if he does not flourish on it, do consult with your GP or Health Visitor or Babies' Clinic. I know of several cases of obstinate eczema (none, it so happens, in an adopted child) where the cure turned out to be a diet of goat's milk and, later, the avoidance of eggs and all normal dairy products.

In addition to milk, Jo may enjoy occasional orange juice or "Haliborange", boiled water or a sip of gripe-water, from a very early age. It is now acceptable to offer "solids" to infants as young as two or three months, i.e. long before most of them have any teeth. With their usual flexibility, most babies will accept this addition to their diet – after, perhaps, initial rejection or hesitation – just as in other times and other climes infants used to thrive, unprotestingly, on an exclusively liquid diet, until they had acquired some teeth – or a younger sibling.

The milk in the bottle should be warm: not hot and not ice-cold or tepid. Hold Jo comfortably in the crook of your arm (you should both be comfortable and relaxed) with him halfway between a sitting and a lying position. Make sure that the bottle is adjusted at the correct angle throughout the feed: if you do not tip it progressively more steeply as the milk disappears, Jo may be taking in gulps of air with the milk – or, even, *instead of* the milk – and this may cause trouble with wind.

Even if he sucks consistently and successfully, he will need to be "burped", i.e. to have his wind brought up, once or twice in the course of his feed. This procedure involves holding him more upright, against your chest so that his head is near yours but facing the other way, and gently patting or rubbing his back until he burps. He may well resent the removal of the teat from his mouth but, with practice on both sides, he will learn the relief that comes with a burp or two and settle down to the rest of his bottle with renewed enthusiasm. He will need burping again at the end of the feed. The little "ugh" that he eventually emits comes to be strangely satisfying to you – partly because it spells success and partly because you enjoy the relief of tension in Jo's body.

The size of the hole in the teat is important. If the hole is too large Jo will be taking in too much milk with each suck. He may then make slight choking noises, milk will begin coming out of his mouth as well as going into it, and you may receive a little shower of milk and saliva on your lap. You will then wish to replace the teat with one that has a smaller hole. If, on the other hand, the hole is too tiny, or is flattened or bunged-up, Jo will suck unavailingly and frustratedly. In order to enlarge the hole, you pierce it with a needle that has been held in a flame for a few seconds to sterilise it. Sometimes a teat goes flat – in which event, however hard Jo works, he will get no milk until it has been righted.

The bottles themselves should be sterilised before use. This is easily done by placing them in an appropriate receptacle containing water and any one of the medically approved sterilising fluids suitable for babies. The simplest way to organise Jo's meals at this early stage is to prepare, once a day, six bottles, complete with milk and teats, and have them ready, standing upright in the cold sterilising liquid. To begin with, Jo will probably have six feeds a day, at about 6.00 a.m., 10.00 a.m., 2.00 p.m., 6.00 p.m. and 10.00 p.m. While very young, he may also need a seventh one at about 2.00 a.m. but this he will soon drop.

He will make it clear to you, after some weeks, which meal he wishes to omit. If you are lucky, it will be the one at 6.00 a.m. But if he elects to sleep through the night – omitting the 10.00 p.m. bottle – I think it best to bow to his wishes and be prepared to feed him at about 6.00 a.m.

This leads us to the first controversial issue: regular meals versus feeding-on-demand. The latter school of thought is probably the more popular today and it has had a long innings. Its proponents argue that Jo knows when he needs nourishment; that if he is crying,

134

there is a cause for it, and that the cause is probably hunger; that the imposition of four-hourly intervals is arbitrary and is imposed by adults for their convenience; and that the child has such a lot to contend with, in addition to the trauma of birth, that we should do all we can to ease his burdens for him.

On the other hand, those in favour of regular meal-times argue as follows. There are a variety of reasons why Jo cries: these include wet or dirty nappies; a desire for attention; pain caused, for instance, by tummy-ache or a sore bottom, or teething troubles – or even a pin sticking into him; and others, including hunger. If Jo is fed every time he cries, the actual cause of distress may go undetected. Moreover, Jo needs to learn when he is ready for food and he cannot begin to learn this if he is never permitted to sense the onset of hunger. If he is allowed to get used to a four-hourly schedule, he will soon adapt to this, physiologically and psychologically, and he will actively look forward to his feeds and have a keener appetite for them.

My own attitude lies somewhat between these two extremes, but it is closer to the second than to the first doctrine. I would not advocate a rigid adherence to the suggested times: if, for instance, 7.30 a.m., 11.30 a.m., etc., happens to suit your household better than 6.00, 10.00, etc., Jo will amenably settle down to this. Nor do I feel that obsessively accurate timekeeping is necessary, or even desirable – whatever the schedule may be. If Jo is asleep at a meal-time, I see no reason to wake him on the dot in order to feed him. If he is still sleeping fifteen–twenty minutes later, I would probably pick him up, talk to him and fondle him and, when he is awake and ready, offer him the warmed bottle. If he is very sleepy, he may suck dreamily and then doze off, having taken very little of the milk. In that event, he may well feel over-hungry long before his next feed is due.

Again, if he starts crying shortly before his official meal-time, I see no objection to feeding him early – provided you ensure that his fretting is not due to some other cause. Go and talk to him; check whether his nappy needs changing; dandle him or change his position in his cot; or let him lie naked on his rug – providing the room-temperature is warm enough and you can stay with him, to see that he doesn't roll too close to the fire-guard or against some sharp object, and that the family pet – if you have one – does not lick his face or lie on him.

Feeding Jo at fairly regular intervals, rather than on demand, does confer certain benefits on the adults caring for Jo – but such benefits, I have repeatedly observed, repercuss favourably on the child. Mother

135

(or father or parent-figure) does not have to be always on the *qui vive*, ready to heat the milk to the required warmth – to find, perhaps, that less than half the amount is imbibed. Parents learn that food is not the be-all and end-all for Jo, even at a few weeks of age. And Jo himself learns, from an early age, that one sometimes has to wait in life for one's needs to be fulfilled and, equally important, that they *will be fulfilled* in due course. (The latter, of course, may not always happen in later life! But if Jo is an adopted child, it will probably take many years before he has to learn this harder lesson.)

There is an added advantage too if, by some chance, Jo's meal is delayed; if, for example, he is out with his parents and they are held up by traffic or friends, they may get home half an hour or more, late. If Jo is used to being fed as soon as he intimates his readiness for a meal, he is likely to be yelling agitatedly by the time home is reached. He may have a real tantrum (more about these in Chapter XVIII) and his parents will be upset and worried – and, illogically, more convinced than ever that feeding-on-demand is best for Jo.

When the time comes to supplement the milk with solids, do not expect Jo to change his habits all at once. He may reject *all* solids at first: neatly expelling them from his mouth by swiftly thrusting out his tongue with the morsel of food on the end of it. Incidentally, offer him a very little on his baby-spoon to start with: learning to cope with a whole mouthful of food takes time and practice. He may exhibit a preference for the sweeter foods, such as liquidised banana or custard over the savoury foods, such as chicken or cauliflower mousse (or, conversely, some infants actively prefer savouries to sweets). Just persevere gently, putting very small spoonfuls of food into his mouth and not offering more until he has swallowed (or expectorated) the last mouthful. If he continues in his refusal, do not persist more than three or four times at one meal; and do not offer him another solid instead, during this feed.

There are, I think, four good principles to follow in the feeding of babies and young children – and, indeed, the not-so-young. (a) Do not force any child to eat what he does not want. It will not do him any good; he may even succeed in vomiting it; and it may induce in him a long-term dislike for that particular foodstuff. But (b) do not offer him some other food instead, at that meal. If he is firm in his refusal, he will probably be healthily hungry at his next meal-time – when he may be offered something different. (c) Never give Jo the impression that you are worried about any reluctance to eat. Never let him feel that by eating he is doing you a favour! On the contrary, if he feels that you are doing *him* a favour in feeding him or giving him a second helping, that is fine. (d) Do not *over*-feed Jo. I have known more than one mother say of her infant, "He's really getting too fat, and they say so at the Clinic too" – and continue to ply him with every mouthful that he can be persuaded to accept. Over-fat babies tend to grow into over-fat toddlers and these, in turn, often become over-weight children and teenagers, who will not thank you when they begin to consider "cosmetic" aspects of their appearance. The middle-weight (in relation to height, of course), like the middle way, is best for Jo.

If these principles are followed, Jo will probably have a good appetite throughout childhood and later, and will tend to enjoy whatever is offered. These last few paragraphs apply to the toddler and older child rather than to the babe-in-arms but, in child-rearing, consistency is desirable: it is wise to begin as you mean to go on – whatever the area of concern.

XIV
Toilet-Training

It seems very fitting that an abundance of hot air should be generated on the topic of excretion! Voices are raised, tempers are lost, passions run high – and, whatever the method used, a few individuals remain bedwetters, some up to their teens and, still fewer, throughout life. I had purchased a uni-sex chamber-pot along with nappies, bottles, baby clothes and cot, once the Adoption Society had finally promised me a baby. But, having carefully perused the literature, I had decided to postpone introducing Jo to the potty until she was six–twelve months old.

However, Miss May, the very experienced social worker who brought me Joanna, explained otherwise. She first helped me to undress and re-dress the seven-week baby – for we both felt that I needed the practice. Miss May then instructed me on the current mode of nappy-pinning; and, to my relief, supervised me while I gave Jo her first bottle in her new home (the Nanny was not due for ten days). During this feeding Miss May said, in her kind, brisk voice, "And you'll put her on the pot of course, as soon as she's finished her bottle." I gasped and said, *"At seven weeks?"* "Oh yes, they're clean little things," asserted Miss May, with less than her customary accuracy.

I took her advice and duly settled Jo on the potty, on my lap, as soon as she had finished her bottle and had been burped – and, to my astonishment, she performed. Miss May looked delighted and said, "You can often catch them like that, just after a feed," and reiterated her injunction to pot the child immediately after every bottle. Her advice turned out to be worthwhile, and I have long remained grateful to her.

My various Nannies were not always keen on the idea, some of them having been indoctrinated with the theory that early potting does no good and may even do harm. But when they learned that it was the social worker's plan rather than mine, and when they saw that it resulted in fewer nappies to wash, they generally proved persuadable. In fact, a year later, it worked far less efficiently with Jonathan than it had with Joanna, but this did not worry any of us. It meant that there was no unwelcome day for Jonathan – at six or twelve or twenty-four months – when he was suddenly presented with a new object and asked to comply with its demands.

The fashion of introducing the child to a chamber-pot late rather than early is understandable in the light of the tendency among child-educators to leap from extreme to extreme. Time was when babies were *expected* to be clean and dry around one and a half–two years. In practice, some made it sooner and some later. But if they failed to fulfil these expectations, they would in some cases be scolded or even punished. In due course, it was realised that this had exactly the opposite effect from the one intended. The child would become fearful; fear begets tension; and tension very often produces loose bowels and/or a release or urine (and, in some cases, constipation).

As ever, a middle way produces best results, i.e. less trouble for both child and adult. I have seen a number of toddlers (of both sexes) drumming their feet furiously on the floor, screaming with rage, when placed on a potty. More than once, I have seen them passionately refuse the chamber-pot and then promptly urinate or defecate in their pants. This is readily comprehensible in a child who has been happily excreting into her nappies throughout her short life and is now presented with a new object – not a toy – with apparently arbitrary demands.

In line with Miss May's dictum, I would offer four recommendations on the subject of toilet-training. (a) Always put Jo on to the potty, on your lap, as soon as she has emitted her final burp. She may or may not perform. Never mind if she doesn't! You will support her and cuddle her and chat with her as she sits enthroned, and this is enjoyable for you both. Do not keep her thus seated for too long. If potting her does not work at first, no harm is done. Jo gets used to the feel of the potty and associates it with the pleasant experiences of fondling and chatting. When it does work, this means a nappy or two less to wash and the gradual building up of a habit that pleases both child and adult.

(b) Nappies should be absolutely bone dry and should be changed frequently – *whenever* Jo is damp, wet or dirty. Disposable nappies are not cheap but they are very helpful when taking Jo to stay with friends, or on a camping holiday. There is no need for "nappy rash" to occur: save for exceptional circumstances, it is caused by Jo's nappy not being changed often enough, or using slightly damp nappies, or failing to dry Jo's bottom thoroughly after her bath or her wash. All babies' skins are tender – some more so than others. End her toilette with a little shower of baby talcum powder, before putting the clean nappy on her.

(c) Do *not* express displeasure if she does not use her pot. She may well perform beautifully after six feeds in a row and then cease to do so. Don't be surprised; don't feel disappointed; just carry on.

Follow the same tactics at night-time. "Pot" the child last thing at night and then put on the clean nappies. If she is wet or dirty in the morning, do not complain or scold – or even frown! This is a natural stage that will probably pass in due course. There is no objection to registering *pleasure* when Jo is clean and dry first thing in the morning or when she uses her potty, as hoped. But she should not feel that she has failed, or that you are disappointed, or cross with her, if she has not yet acquired this skill.

I am using the feminine pronoun, "she", as it is Jo's turn here to be female. But it is worth mentioning that boys do tend to be clean and dry somewhat later than girls. As with every rule there are exceptions to this. Nonetheless, it is worth bearing in mind: if your Jonathan is still wetting his bed at three years of age, do not despair! If you do not worry about it, *he* will not worry; and if he doesn't worry, he will grow out of it, in due course.

When a child is still bed-wetting at this stage, it is a good idea to pick him up and pot him just before you go to bed – be this at 10.0, 11.0 or midnight. He will scarcely wake up but will probably pass water in a semi-sleeping state and, once tucked up again, will return to a sound sleep.

(d) Constipation. I favour the view that the child should have a bowel-movement at least once a day. I learned from my young Nannies – some straight from Nursery Nurse training – that this is an "oldfashioned idea", that "the baby is *not constipated* if she goes a few days without having a motion". They said it loud, clear and dogmatically, as though reciting a lesson – as, indeed, they probably were. But, having witnessed the discomfort even fear of toddlers who are told to "push hard" when having trouble in defecating, I hold equally dogmatically the opposing view.

I advocate giving Jo a mild laxative, such as milk-of-magnesia tablets or liquid, as soon as one day has gone by without her having passed a motion, but do not express (or feel) anxiety when she fails to perform – and do not keep her too long on the potty. The taking of a laxative should ensure that she will not experience any pain or discomfort on this score and that she will not take against doing "big job". It also has the virtue of inculcating regular bowel-movements probably for the rest of her life – a useful habit!

I had to employ a Nanny when my children were young because I had to remain in full-time employment – which I much enjoyed – in order to support them (and myself). Thus there were always two people with whom Jo felt equally at ease – which is not always the case in one-parent families (or even, sometimes, in two-parent families!). The occasions when Nanny and I clashed were not very frequent, partly because we naturally boxed and coxed, but when serious dissension did occur, I insisted on having my way. I learned a good deal from my succession of Nannies and some of them learned a little from me. They were generous enough to volunteer this when, in the years to come, I visited them and their offspring or they brought their children to see me. But we all learned most from the children themselves. They have a way of making it clear when they are ready for the next stage – whatever this may be.

I usually took over from Nanny at the weekends, and in the evenings from about 5.30 onwards. Moreover, when Jo first joined me, she and I had ten days together before our first Nanny was able to join us. This proved an excellent thing as it gave me the requisite confidence and Jo seemed to realise from that time that I was her Mum. She soon learned to accept us both, however, and once a child feels equally secure with two different people, she finds it easier to accept others, as and when the need arises. This became very clear as Nannies came and Nannies went – without disturbing Joanna's and Jonathan's life or lessening their capacity, in adolescence and later, to form strong lasting emotional ties.

I believe it to be very important for the baby (and the child) to be relaxed and happy with at least two different people – but, preferably, with three or four. Then when the mother-figure is ill or has to go away or is giving birth to another child, this is not a traumatic event for Jo. She will cheerfully spend her time with one of the other familiar adults whom she loves; she will be less upset if, for any reason, she herself has to leave home for a short time; and she will be far less likely to be tense or "difficult" with guests or with a new baby-

141

sitter. Some experts have decreed that the mother/child link is unique and indissoluble – and, hence, that the mother should become a full-time slave to the infant. This practice is just as bad for the child as it is for the parent. Apart from the practical problems inevitably raised, it tends to cause over-dependence on Jo's part and, ultimately, resentment (often unrecognised) on the part of the mother.

XV
Sleeping Habits

A baby's sleep-routine is an important part of his upbringing: partly because young things need plenty of sleep and the pattern laid down in early youth may persist into childhood and adolescence; and partly because the adults in the family also have *their* needs. If these are ignored, not only do the adults become short-tempered and fatigued, and liable to feel that "one child is enough" (which is hard on Jo), but their ill-humour repercusses on the child. A certain measure of enlightened self-interest on the part of parents is desirable. Indeed I sometimes feel, when reading or hearing of child-abuse, that tragedy might have been averted if the parents had shown earlier a little more foresight, more strength of mind – in a sense, more selfishness. It is surely not the *sound* of a baby's crying and screaming for hours that upsets the adults, in these days of all-pervading "music", motor cycles, etc. – it is the irritation and guilt felt by the parents because the child is unhappy. These emotions build up and may sometimes contribute, I suspect, to the phenomenon of baby-battering.

Decide on a nightly routine for Jo and try to keep to it throughout infancy and well into childhood. It will prove beneficial for him as well as for you. The actual time you choose for bed does not really matter. It will probably be some time between 6.0 and 9.0 p.m. – determined by such factors as when your spouse (and perhaps yourself) gets home from work, when you wish to get Jo up in the morning, how much sleep he needs (this varies considerably), what time you have your evening meal, and when Jo has his bath.

I liked my children to bath in the evening because this enabled me to bath them myself or, if I was late home, to join in at the drying stage. Most babies grow to enjoy their bath, if the water is warm but

143

not too hot and the soap does not get into their eyes. The evening is usually a more leisurely time than the morning, allowing more time for water-play – with ducks or boats or a floating ball. Jo will learn to love his water-play from the age of a few months, and he should not be hurried over it.

After a little while, however, it must come to an end. A good ploy for persuading a child to stop whatever he is doing, when he wishes to continue doing it – and childhood is full of such situations – is the 1-2-3 method. Thus, when Jo has had a good splashy game with his favourite duck, for instance, you say THREE MORE! and fly the duck out of the water on to his shoulder, saying ONE! Back goes the duck into the bath and you repeat the process, saying TWO! And finally, after the third duck-flight on to Jo's shoulder, saying THREE!, you whisk Jo out of the bath, well-wrapped in his towel and begin drying him – perhaps to the accompaniment of a nursery rhyme. We used to have a special "Rubadub-dub" song for drying.

This technique may not work for the first few times if Jo is very keen on staying in the bath, but after a bit he will get used to it; he will know that "1-2-3" marks the end of bath-time; and he will grow to accept this. It is less of a shock than suddenly being removed from the comfortable warmth and the fascinating water-play.

The 1-2-3 method is useful also in other situations, such as stopping a favourite game or going into the arms of someone new. Jo may have been playing Peep-bo – his companion's face momentarily being hidden behind hand or newspaper, and then suddenly reappearing with a smiling BO! – or he may have been delightedly tossed in the air and caught several times or briefly turned upside-down and then quickly held right-way-up again. These games cannot continue indefinitely as the breathless adult well realises, but young Jo does not yet understand this. He soon learns, however, that 1-2-3 is a warning of impending closure and, hence, ending the game – whatever it may be – becomes less of a blow and more acceptable.

Secondly, this method teaches Jo that the magic syllables herald *a change* in the situation – such as going to an unfamiliar person. A child-loving (or ingratiating) visitor, say, Mrs Ivy, will often put out her arms for Jo at an early meeting; and Jo may find himself swiftly and unceremoniously handed over, like a parcel, to the guest. Many babies dislike this, understandably, and they register their disapproval by crying or struggling – to the dismay of Mrs Ivy ("but I always get on so well with babies") and the regret of the parent. Jo can be prepared for the temporary take-over by means of the 1-2-3 technique. If you want your visitor to have the pleasure of holding the baby, swing the arm-held Jo towards her with a "ONE!" and swing him back to yourself; then again with a "TWO!" and back; and finally with a long, melodious "THREEEE!" swing him into Mrs Ivy's expectant arms. (If she is not used to babies, get her to sit down in advance.)

The method has its uses, thirdly, when Jo is *not* enthralled with what he is doing. If, for example, you would like him to finish his pudding, in which he is losing interest, try saying, "Just three more spoonfuls – 1 . . . 2 . . . 3" – and stop after "3", even if his plate is not empty. Jo will understand and will probably co-operate, if you do desist in accordance with your implicit promise.

He may even start using the method himself – which leads us to the fourth advantage: this technique marks the beginning of simple counting and, when Jo reaches toddler-stage, he will happily go on to four, five, six, etc., when climbing stairs, for instance, hand-in-hand with you, having got the idea both of counting and of three-ness.

Another habit that Jo may have adopted by the time he is two or three – if you begin instilling it earlier – is to put his hand in front of his mouth when he coughs or sneezes. Your friends may think it rather a joke if you say to a twelve–eighteen-month-old Jo, when he is coughing, "Put your hand in front of your mouth," and you place his hand in position for him, but it isn't just a joke. Jo will regard it as a game at first and then, as he grows older, he will tend to do it as a matter of course.

The habit of saying "please" and "thank you" is in a similar category. If you would like Jo to be saying these words, appropriately, at two-three years of age, you should use these terms, at suitable times, to Jo himself, as you would with an older person; and remember that – for obvious reasons – it is far easier to teach someone to say "please" than to say "thank you". But do not expect him to say "please" for something he does not really want! In due course he will say both, automatically, if those around him use the words and if he has been encouraged to do so from early days.

Let us now return to Jo – who has been out of the bath for the last few minutes, on your knee, well-wrapped in a warm towel, being briskly rubbed. After-the-bath is a good time for a last cuddle, a last meal (followed by teeth-brushing – at first as a sort of game, with pleasant-tasting toothpaste), perhaps a little rough-and-tumble or a few nursery-rhymes. When Jo reaches one and a half or two years of age, he will begin to enjoy looking at picture books with you or watching you draw pictures for him. A few months later, he will like

145

listening to stories told by you, or read aloud to him; and, surprisingly soon, he will be correcting you if, in a familiar story, you alter the wording!

His pleasure in watching television will also be developing. But that is something that he can enjoy alone and when he is older. The great virtue of playing and story-telling and romping together is that these are done *with you*. They help to cement the affection between you and to induce concentration. They give joy to you both, and each is dependent on the other for this job.

Then a goodnight kiss and, "1-2-3 TO BED." Jo probably will not relish the idea of ending the fun and of losing your company. You pick him up gently and, holding him close, you put him into his cot: lay him on his side – with *no pillow* in infancy (to avoid danger of suffocation) – and tuck him up firmly so that he feels securely held. Turn off the light and shut the door: young babies are not afraid of the dark. If they have always had a dark bedroom, they take it for granted. And, in that event, they are unlikely to develop a fear of the dark when older – unless, of course, it is suggested to them. Well-meaning adults are quite capable of saying, "*You're* not afraid of the dark, are you?" thus unwittingly instilling the idea.

When you put Jo to bed and close the door, he may wail. This is only natural since he likes company and he has been enjoying himself. But do not re-enter the room – or turn on the light, or open the door – until silence has reigned for, say, fifteen–twenty minutes. Then, if you need reassurance – as I certainly did and most mothers do, especially with their first child – creep in and listen to the comforting sound of Jo's even breathing. (The feeling, outside his room, that "if he cries he is unhappy and if he is silent he must be dead" does eventually pass!)

You can shut the door again: the belief that mothers hear the slightest cry from their child, even through closed doors, is no myth but is perfectly true. Whether you are engaged in animated conversation or watching a noisy film on television or are, yourself, fast asleep, you will be immediately alert to the slightest sound uttered by Jo. It is an interesting phenomenon, equally true for adoptive mothers and biological mothers.

If Jo once learns that by crying when left alone, he will get you back – even temporarily – he will, of course, exert his authority. And thus is initiated a vicious circle: he cries when left; you go to him, in effect rewarding his crying. The next night you may say, after having put

146

him to bed, "Oh no, I shan't go to him: he must learn . . ." But it is *you* who must learn.

Once Jo realises that bedtime is bedtime, that there is nothing to do but sleep once he has been put down, he will not wail when left – unless, of course, there is something wrong. Let him have a favourite plaything in bed with him – perhaps a teddy-bear or some other soft toy that he likes – and do allow him to suck his thumb (or other fingers) if he is so inclined. Jo's thumb is better for him than a "dummy", partly because the former is more likely to be clean, and partly because Jo always has it with him! If he is accustomed to using a dummy, he will naturally be perturbed when it falls out of his reach.

My Joanna and Jonathan both sucked their thumbs, sometimes during the day and always when going to sleep. When they reached two to two and a half years of age, I asked them to try to stop thumb-sucking when they were up and about (this was helped by my ensuring that they always had something congenial to do), but I added that I had no objection to their continuing the habit when going to sleep. This system worked very well: after a few months, they ceased thumb-sucking during the day but they continued the habit in bed for a year or two and it appeared to have an almost hypnotic effect on them. A baby treated like this from the start – left on his own, warm dry and comfortable, with a favourite soft toy and perhaps sucking thumb or fingers – tends to go to sleep quickly and to sleep soundly; or, if he is one of those infants who needs little sleep – and such do exist – he may babble contentedly to himself. *If* something is amiss, however, such as his having an ear-ache or a soiled nappy, then he will let you know and you will naturally go to his aid.

A child who cries as soon as he is left on his own probably has nothing the matter with him – except desire for company; and this he can learn to overcome only with your help. If he is in genuine trouble or pain, his cry sounds different (you will soon learn to tell the difference) and it will probably not arise the moment you leave him.

Once Jo has got into the habit of accepting solitude and darkness at bedtime and throughout the night – which can be managed if you are consistent – you and he will both reap the benefit. He will accept that you (or another parent-figure) determine when it is time for bed, *not* he; and he will not get over-tired – a childhood condition that may lead, paradoxically, to difficulty in falling asleep (yet another vicious circle). Moreover, you will not suffer from tension, mixed with resentment-cum-guilt. And when you and your husband want to go out for the evening, you will be able to use a baby-sitter secure in the knowledge that both Jo and the sitter will have an undisturbed evening. On no account should Jo ever be left alone in the house, by night or day. Nor should he be left alone in a car.

Most of the above advice concerns Jo as a baby of a few months. But it is wise to continue along the same lines – except that pre-bed stories will grow longer and bedtime will grow later. If, however, you lose your consistency and allow Jo to take command of the situation a year or two later, instead of hearing a wail, you will observe the sitting-room door being opened and hear a two- or three-year-old voice innocently requesting a drink of water, or complaining of a tummy-ache. By this time Jo knows exactly what will be considered reasonable grounds for disturbing you; and he will *continue to produce them for the next few years!*

Such visitations are especially liable to happen when you have friends in for the evening; and – however smilingly they may protest that Jo is very sweet and they enjoy seeing him – it is better for Jo (and probably preferable for your guests) if night-time is regarded as *adult-time*, by the entire household. A child who takes it for granted that bedtime spells SLEEP-TILL-MORNING is happier, healthier and more popular than one who manipulates the grown-ups. This acceptance pays dividends, too, if you are unwell, or if you and Jo have to separate for some reason, or if Jo gets some childhood complaint. He will be far less upset by such happenings – and they are bound to occur – if his routine does not demand your being on tap at every hour of the day and night.

The main burden of this chapter has been insistence on a regular routine or basic framework for Jo, at night-time. Interestingly enough, the existence of such a routine actually facilitates flexibility on those occasions when this is needed. But it is not only at night that regularity is desirable. In my view, all babies and young children thrive better if brought up within a certain framwork. This, therefore, is the theme of the next chapter.

XVI
The Need for a Framework

An attitude has grown up during the last few decades that the child must be allowed to develop "naturally", without let or hindrance from adults: that, even in infancy, Jo should be allowed the maximum possible freedom and should never be thwarted – unless she is about to do herself (or some other child) actual bodily harm. The psychological harm that this may do to Jo or her companions seems rarely to be considered – until too late.

This attitude has been fostered largely by psychologists and psychoanalysts and even, to some extent, by certain educationists (mainly those who do not have a great deal to do with children, in practice). The theory is that the child should be encouraged to unfold, like a flower, petal by petal, until full bloom is reached. According to this school of thought, no discipline should be imposed from without because self-discipline is best and this comes from within. Jo must not be forced to do anything she does not wish to do, nor must she be prevented from doing what she does want to do – whatever form her enterprises may take and however much these may frustrate or annoy the adults or siblings (or family pets) in the vicinity. If she demands attention from her mother or mother-figure, she must receive this at once, whatever conversation or activity her mother may be engaged in at the time. She should virtually never be gainsaid and should not be punished or scolded, since this might arouse feelings of guilt or shame – and this, it is suggested, must be avoided at all costs since it might have a deleterious effect on the adolescent or adult Jo.

It is the extreme opposite of the old precept – equally pernicious to my mind – that children should be seen and not heard; that their "spirit should be broken" in an endeavour to repress the natural

149

noisiness, exuberance and curiosity of childhood; and that all should conform to the same rigid, predictable pattern of behaviour. This was a far from wholesome ideal and it is well that, in most families, it is no longer considered desirable.

To leap to the other extreme, however, and to equate licence with liberty or "creativity" or "inner discipline" is foolish and self-defeating. Jo needs a certain framework within which to live – and perhaps, a few years later, against which to rebel. It need not be *the same* framework for all families, but all children need one of some kind, and its implementation should not be left until the last possible moment.

Self-discipline is indeed to be aimed at but this will not be achieved without earlier *external* control. Awareness of sensations of guilt or shame is a prerequisite for consciousness of a sense of right and wrong. And if this awareness is not instilled in infancy and early childhood it will be intolerable for Jo when it hits her – as it inevitably will – when she is older. So standards need to be laid down from early days, whether they concern manners (basically the appreciation of someone else's point of view), or the law of the land (concerning, for instance, arson, theft or vandalism). A child brought up in complete absence of rules and regulations is not only egotistic and selfish: she rapidly becomes unpopular with both peers and elders – and, hence, miserable.

It is sometimes claimed that example is what is required: that if the parents behave in the way they would like Jo to behave, this is enough. It is of course *necessary* that parents should act kindly, honestly and justly, if these are the kinds of quality they desire in their offspring, but it is *not sufficient*. In any case, the Indulgence School of thought (to coin a phrase) inevitably results in one-sidedness. If the parents are constantly "giving", the child is forced into the position of constantly "taking". Their example, therefore, is scarcely one which the child has the option of immediately following.

Moreover, many children, when they reach more mature years, state explicitly that they had wished for guidance and some degree of imposed control. Phyllis Crabtree, it may be remembered, ". . . equated discipline with love: if people cared about you, then they tried to make you better people" (page 40). And I recall the child of a psychoanalyst – observing another boy being smacked by his mother – exclaiming wistfully, "She must love him very much to *punish* him."

I have vivid recollections of a number of sons and daughters brought up on the Indulgence model. They tend to show symptoms

150

of insecurity, such as crying frequently, sleeping badly, requiring constant attention, being intolerant of other children, wetting their beds after three or four years of age and finding it insupportable to be separated from Mum. Since they are inevitably disobedient, their freedom has to be markedly more restricted than that of their coevals. Such children are usually very late in achieving independence. They cannot "be trusted" at three or four not to break glass, not to strike matches or not to walk into the garden pond (I know of one well-loved child who drowned in this way); or, at six or seven, to remain on the pavement – hence having to be held firmly by the hand.

I well remember a set of twins, Joey and Jolyon, aged just under two when, years ago, I spent a long weekend with them and their parents – a never-to-be-forgotten experience! They had been brought up on the Indulgence principle, the father being a busy industrialist who left domestic matters to his wife. She was a gentle, modest, sweet-natured woman who had read the then current edicts by experts on child-rearing and had steadfastly followed them. The boys were pale, restless and tired-looking for they did not get enough sleep, and they were extremely fussy about their food. They could not be left alone together as they fought constantly – using not only hands, feet, nails and teeth but any available hard object. On the Saturday afternoon we all went to tea with a family consisting of parents, a three-year-old boy and a one-year-old girl. The twins bashed their young hosts over the head, until forcibly restrained. They then rode the three-year-old's wooden tricycle round and round the room at high speed, grinding small toys into the carpet. They declined most of the appetising tea provided but vigorously flung the food around. They were aggressively unco-operative in response to all suggestions of games, actively interfering if anyone else began playing.

This may sound like fun – for the twins – but they *did not enjoy themselves*. Nor, of course, did the other children. It became clear that Joey and Jolyon would never again be invited to that household nor, indeed, to any other where they had once received hospitality. When they got home they were bathed – separately, as they fought whenever they shared a bath. And when they were put into their dropside cots (on opposite sides of the room) they began the ritual head-thumping against the wooden head-boards which, I was told, went on every evening, sometimes for an hour or more. They banged rhythmically but not in unison. I was invited to feel the backs of their heads and I found a large lump of hardened skin on each child's head as a result of the repeated thumping.

The twins were unhappy most of the time and so were their parents. It was a household without peace, harmony or any possibility of relaxing. The lack of framework had resulted in the children having absolutely no concept of give-and-take or of obedience: indeed, they scarcely heard what was said to them. I did not keep in touch with the family but there can be no doubt that Joey and Jolyon had a hard time when they went to school – and that they gave their teachers and their schoolmates a hard time.

More recently I entertained a three-year-old girl and her parents – who, also, were steadfastly against imposing any form of retribution. Thus, Jilly declined most of what she was offered at lunch – and threw what she accepted on to the floor, or spread it over her place-mat. During our afternoon walk, she flung her jacket into the river and she began spitting at people. At tea, when offered the choice of milk, weak tea or orange-juice, she demanded coffee, helped herself to three biscuits at once and finished none of them; and, when allowed to get down, she went to the window and, very neatly, bit a hole in the net curtain!

All these feats were performed with a keen, challenging eye on her parents – as though begging them to react, other than with a mild, "Really, darling!" When, finally, I took a tough line (saying firmly, "NO!" and, "STOP THAT, Jill!") she appeared relieved; she did stop; and she volunteered to her parents on the drive home that she had had a lovely time. She was, in fact, rarely taken out to friends, as her parents were scared of her probable behaviour. Their social life naturally suffered too and, wherever they went, they were in a perpetual state of tension.

It is often said that two to three years is a particularly difficult age from a parent's point of view. This is true if no framework has already been established, for by the age of two Jo is very mobile, is "into everything" and – as her parents are wont to declare, often with pride – "She has a will of her own." *All* young things have a will of their own, unless it has been crushed out of them in infancy – a fate that no reader of this book would wish upon any child. But ensuring that at the word NO, Jo stops doing what she had in mind – whether this was putting her fingers into an electric socket or eating gravel or pulling the cat's tail – is *not* the same thing as crushing a child or breaking her spirit. If she has been treated consistently and rationally since she was a few weeks old, by the time she is two she will already have learned to co-operate; and she can therefore be granted a great deal more freedom than the child who has habitually been allowed every

152

possible licence, and who suddenly gains the impression that everything she wishes to do now is discouraged and that everywhere she wants to go is out of bounds.

What do I mean by "a framework"? – rewarding acceptable behaviour and penalising unacceptable behaviour? Yes, up to a point, but that would be an over-simplication. It is far from being the whole story. I do not subscribe wholeheartedly to the Behaviourist ethos, for this treats human beings (to say nothing of the lower animals) as mechanical entities: as unthinking, unfeeling objects to be manipulated by "superior", equally insentient, almost equally mechanistic beings. I have recorded in detail my critique of Behaviourism as the psychological be-all and end-all, elsewhere.*

I say "as the be-all and end-all" since it would clearly be absurd to reject *in toto* the rewarding, or reinforcing, of what is deemed desirable or the penalising of what is deemed undesirable. Such strategy is as old as infant-rearing itself; it dates from the beginning of time and is employed by the parents of many species – not just man and certainly not just psychologists! But this "conditioning process" is not enough. It is too inflexible and too specific, omitting the atmosphere of the home in which the child is reared – intangible and all-pervasive; omitting, too, the role of example by parents, siblings and other companions.

The theory neglects also the *genetic* contribution to behaviour and to character-formation. As is evident in the first part of the book, this contribution is quite considerable; and it plays an ever-increasing role in the development of an individual who is allowed ever-increasing freedom. Such freedom – once a framework has been accepted – is essential if the child is to realise her full potential in adolescence and adulthood, and this fulfilment is surely the aim of a loving parent.

The theory of Conditioning stems largely from Pavlov's physiological work with the lower animals† and J.B. Watson's brash statement of the principles of Behaviourism. Watson actually claimed that given a dozen healthy infants and a completely free hand, he would "guarantee to take any one at random and train him to become any type of specialist [he, Watson,] might select – doctor, lawyer, artist, merchant-chief, and yes, even beggar and thief,

---

* Alice Heim, "The Proper Study of Psychology", New Universities Quarterly, 32, 2, 135–154, 1979.
† Pavlov, I.P., *Conditioned Reflexes: an Investigation of the Physiological Activity of the Cerebral Cortex*, Oxford University Press, 1927.

regardless of his talents, penchants, tendencies, abilities, vocations and race of his ancestors."*

It might be thought that experimental psychologists have lost something of their naïvety and their God-playing attitude during the last half-century, but parallel claims are still made – for instance by B.F. Skinner and by Behaviour Therapists, despite their prefacing the term Behaviourism by the word "new" or "neo". It remains essentially similar in its over-simplification, its mechanistic approach and its stress on extrinsic reward and punishment.

One of the aims of setting up a framework such as I have described is to induce *intrinsic* motivation in the child – to play constructively, to communicate, to learn. If Jo does not develop interests and inner resources from an early age, she will find it difficult to do so later. Neither the Indulgence method nor an exclusively Behaviourist technique will teach her concentration or co-operation or enjoyment of a given activity for its own sake. And if Jo has not acquired these, boredom, continual opposition and discontent are liable to ensue – paving the way for what used to be called Delinquency but, in some quarters, is now designated as Individuality, Originality or Creativity!

*Watson, J.B., *Behaviourism*, p. 82, Norton, New York; 1925.

XVII
Two to Five

By the time Jo reaches two to two and a half he can usually say quite a few words and can string some of them together. His recognition vocabulary is of course larger than his spoken vocabulary, i.e. he can understand a great deal more than he can express (as do older people, when conversing in a foreign language). Jo responds to tone of voice and facial expression as well as to the actual words spoken: in this he again resembles his elders but, as he is still feeling his way, he probably depends even more on intonation, emphasis and facial expression than do his seniors – some of whom lose this kind of perceptiveness as they grow older.

During the next three years Jo develops at tremendous speed, not only in communication skills – with people of all ages, including his peers and infants-in-arms (some toddlers are impressively "good with babies") – but in his mobility and physical co-ordination. During these years, Jo goes all the way from progressing in an unsteady wobble with a wide wheel-base and frequent falls to becoming a steady walker, a fleet runner and – if not discouraged by anxious companions – a confident, sure-footed climber.

If toddlers fall when walking or trotting about a room, they tend to fall *well*, that is relaxedly, so that they rarely sprain an ankle or tear a ligament. Their elders have to learn to fall, all over again, if they take up such sports as judo or parachute-jumping, where falling is essential and may well have serious effects if the faller is tense. But the walking toddler does not resist falling as he loses his balance – unless he learns to tense up from the reaction of his companion, probably his mother. Jo does not have as far to fall as an adult has, he feels at home on the floor and he will just flop down – and laugh, and get up again, if he is uninjured and if this is what is expected of him.

So do not rush, volubly sympathising with Jo when he falls down (or bangs his elbow or bumps his head on the table). Laugh with him – for he will take his cue from you – and, if you like, encourage him to smack the table, saying, "Naughty table!" Like the rest of us, Jo may feel angry when hurt, and venting one's rage on some external object is the next best thing to venting it on a living being. A year or two later he may genuinely find it funny to blame an inanimate object for his own clumsiness.

Needless to say, if he has really hurt himself – in which event his cry sounds different and tears will flow – he should of course be comforted and helped to get over it. If he hits his head hard, having fallen down uncarpeted steps for instance, he should lie down quietly for a while; and if he vomits after such an incident, consult your doctor in case of concussion, or delayed concussion. If he is completely silent after a bad fall, there may indeed be cause for anxiety and for medical advice.

In general, the two–five-year-old is tough and takes vicissitudes for granted, unless he has been "taught" to fuss. Of course he must be protected from traffic, from sharp spikes or broken glass, and from falling out of the window or down a cliff. He should, moreover, not be lovingly dragged by enthusiastic parents to the more horrific and challenging sideshows at a fair before he is ready for them. But he should be allowed to act out his natural adventurousness and to test his own limits. If he wants to climb trees or a climbing-frame, to use a slide or a see-saw, or walk along the top of a wall or a fallen tree-trunk, do not dissuade him or warn him of the dangers. He should be encouraged in such ventures verbally or with a proffered hand.

On the other hand, the timid child should not be forced into essaying such activities if he is not attracted by them. To do so may put him off physically risky situations for years – in which case he may later suffer at the hands of schoolmates or may, perhaps, never realise the joys (and the occasional uses) of accepting physical challenges. If unforced, the timorous child may take to some of the more hazardous pursuits a year or two later – and highly delighted he will be to find that he can cope with them.

Most children past the age of four to five are reasonably sure-footed and sure-handed, and have an adequate sense of balance. It is unusual for a child to suffer from vertigo when on top of a building or ladder or mountain – unless this is "suggested" to him either by observing a companion who is obviously ill-at-ease or, by a well-meaning adult who keeps issuing warnings: "Hold tight . . . don't lean over . . . go carefully . . . take my hand . . . come away from the edge . . .", etc. On the other hand, the confident young child may not realise that the ground at the edge of a steep hill, for instance, may be treacherous, or that another child might collide with him, accidentally or deliberately, while he is standing at the very edge – with possibly disastrous consequences.

There are many activities, however, untainted by elements of physical risk, which can be enjoyed jointly by parent and child. These include pastimes such as model railways and cars; Russian dolls: inside a doll, inside another doll, inside another . . .; building beakers or bricks and other "constructional toys"; jigsaw puzzles (with a FEW LARGE pieces at this stage); dolls' houses; dressing and undressing dolls and teddy-bears, and bathing those that can stand it; making scrap-books; looking at picture-books; dressing-up.

Equally engrossing but less demanding financially are pastimes such as cat's cradle and "finger see-saw" (both of which need only a piece of string and minimal parental skill); "This is the way the ladies ride", "the railway menu-backwards" and "round about the garden" (the last three requiring only the parent's lap and voice and energy); singing and acting-out nursery-rhymes together; and telling stories. Straitened means certainly need not worry the parents of children at this stage. As many discomfited parents discover at Christmas and birthdays, Jo is apt to settle delightedly to play with his crackling pretty wrapping paper – ignoring the carefully chosen toy which was enfolded within!

Such activities (and I have given just a few examples from the enormous range of possibilities) have the virtue of *being shared* by parent and child and of involving Jo in active collaboration rather than passive observation. Incidentally, they also tend to encourage concentration on Jo's part since they all demand his attention for at least a few consecutive minutes. This will be helpful to him when he goes to nursery school and, eventually, to "real school".

A word of warning here, however! If Jo's Dad happens to enjoy, say, railways, or his Mum loves jigsaw puzzles (or conversely), there is a danger of the parent's taking over the activity – and the fun – from the child. I have more than once been present when a frustrated three-year-old has been saying eagerly, "Let me have a go, Dad" (at running the train or sailing the boat, or whatever), only to be brushed aside by an enthralled father muttering, "Just a moment, Jo," or "Let *me* do this bit" – to the chagrin of Jo, who realises that the game is no

157

longer for his benefit: that he has been relegated to the role of barely tolerated spectator!

This sort of hazard does not apply to play-schools, and these also possess other advantages. Most nursery schools will take children from the age of two and a half or three to five and it is desirable to send Jo to nursery school, especially if he is the first-born. If he is an only child, I think it is essential for him to attend nursery school, otherwise his first experience of "real school" at the age of five may prove quite an unpleasant shock to him. However friendly and companionable Jo's parents may be – walking, talking and playing with him during many of his waking hours – this cannot take the place of being with other children of about his own age, of learning to accept instructions from an initially strange adult and of fitting into an environment other than his own home. All these are important if Jo is to become a happy, adaptable individual, and the earlier he learns about sharing, and taking turns, and appreciating that he is not the centre of the universe, the better for him and his future companions.

If Jo's parents both have full-time jobs, they sometimes place him with a registered child-minder, rather than first a day-nursery and, later, nursery-school. This is a defensible solution provided that the child-minder looks after *several* children and that she is genuinely fond of them and has the vigour, patience and kindness that her task requires. But even so it is, I think, second best. She is unlikely to have either the training of the "teacher" or the variety of facilities possessed by play-schools (I use this word to cover both day-nurseries and nursery-schools).

The latter usually include a sand-pit, finger-paints, appropriate music (to which the children can sing and dance – and listen), a garden for outdoor play, folding beds for the after-lunch rest and a more varied collection of toys, games and books than is generally found in a private house. Moreover, the play-school is prepared for the children to make a mess with their sand, paints, etc., in a way that many parents and child-minders cannot tolerate at home. In "school" Jo learns both to act freely and uninhibitedly – as long as he does not interfere with the freedom and comfort of his mates – and he learns also to help to clear up towards the end of a session. He comes to realise that the latter is necessary and that it can even be enjoyable, especially when done with others. He learns too to form a relationship with several adults whom he does not see at home and with whom he is more intimate than are his parents.

The teachers and the apparatus are good, but best of all for Jo is the presence of his peers. Children teach children, unwittingly. Jo will learn the essence of justice and fair-mindedness, of sharing, of awaiting his turn, of how to stand up for himself and, as he grows in mind and body, how to protect the younger and weaker. Most important, these experiences are not felt as artificial, as imposed by "the grown-ups". They stem from the fact that Jo is surrounded by other children of his own age. Admittedly, the "framework" is there; the teachers are in the background, even during the periods of free play, to ensure that a *Lord of the Flies* situation does not arise.* But for some periods they remain in the background as much as possible, realising the value that children have for one another.

Play-school, however, occupies only some hours of the day and – having made a plea for it – I should like to revert to the family-life of Jo and his parents. The case against the only child has already been made: in the first part of this book both parents and solitary adoptees have expressed their lasting regret at lack of siblings. I should like now to suggest a system which I found valuable from many points of view, but which requires at least two children. This practice consists of having "day-turns".

The age-gap between my Joanna and Jonathan is fifteen months. From the time they were, respectively, four and three years of age, they had their day-turns. Joanna's days were Monday, Wednesday, Friday and alternate Sundays; and Jonathan's days were Tuesday, Thursday, Saturday – and the *other* alternate Sundays. These days applied to "nice *and* nasty things", as they used to put it. Thus on Monday, Wednesday, etc., it was Joanna who offered the sweets after lunch, for instance, who held the lead when walking the dog (which they both liked to do), who helped with the washing-up and emptying the pedal-bin (which did not particularly attract them), and who had first go on the swing (since, as with all children, the moment one of them wanted to use it – having ignored it, perhaps, for weeks – the other urgently and simultaneously wanted a go on it). On Tuesday, Thursday, etc., it was Jonathan who did these things – and, of course, others; it was he who had first choice on his days and whose vote outweighed Joanna's if they each wanted to play a different, incompatible game.

These examples may sound very trivial. Indeed they *are* trivial from the vantage-point of an adult, but they are the sorts of things that matter passionately to a young child. I instituted day-turns because I

*Golding, William, *Lord of the Flies*, Faber & Faber, 1954.

had so often witnessed the sons and daughters of my friends coming to blows and tears over just such matters. The arrangement is specially useful in the case of some unforeseen nursery-crisis: one has only to state, "but it's *Joanna's* (or Jonathan's) day!" and peace reigns again. The system is fair, and is seen to be fair by the child. I well recall Joanna, aged about six, hopefully asking me one morning, "Is it alternate Sunday today?"

She and Jonathan naturally did have their disputes, but this practice worked sufficiently well to reduce quarrelling substantially and to prompt a number of friends and acquaintances to adopt the procedure. A comparable arrangement can be made if there are three or more children in the family, but its organisation is then slightly more complex! My two continued the practice until they were about ten and eleven, after which it gradually fell into desuetude – though for many years it was invoked for the weekly chore of taking out the dustbins!

Two to three years is rather young to be offered a choice, e.g. "Will you have orange-juice or milk –" "Do you want the corner-seat or would you rather sit here, between Mum and Dad?" "Would you like to go to the loo before we leave?" By all means, give Jo variety – whether of drinks, seats or whatever – but make decisions on his behalf at this tender age, and just *take* him to the loo before you leave the house. The "easy", accommodating two and a half-year-old is sometimes confused by being offered a choice: he may feel flustered, he may seek to give the "right" answer, and he may wish a moment later to revoke whatever decision he made. The "difficult" child is apt to demand tea in reply to the first question and, in response to the second, he elects to stand! His response to the third question is to decline and, later, to wet his pants.

I have often witnessed such scenes and have usually felt that the adults were "asking for it". Making a choice resembles inner discipline in that both must first be imposed from without. When Jo is coming up to four–five years of age, that is the time to offer him alternatives – although I think it preferable that there should be *no* right answer in the mind of the parent when they pose their question.

The reader will have observed that I elicited the help of my children for light household chores from an early age. This is a good idea since, when very young, they *like* to be asked to help: it makes them feel responsible and grown-up. Of course the jobs take much longer and may have to be redone (in privacy) at first – just as encouraging Jo to tie his own shoe-laces and do up his own buttons at three or four takes

160

longer than if you do it for him. But it is well worthwhile for, when the time comes that they could do the chores efficiently, they will be far less keen to help! If, however, they have already acquired the habit, they take it for granted that they should do their share and they continue to do so, without resentment.

Since this chapter is headed "Two to Five" this is perhaps a suitable place in which to discuss the advent of a younger sibling for Jo and its effect on him (although, of course, he may be under two or over five when Josephine arrives). Psychologists have made much of the importance of considering Jo's reaction to a new brother or sister, and this is a topic on which I wholeheartedly agree with my colleagues. Jo will have been the central figure at home throughout his young life. However conscientiously (or egotistically) his parents will at times have ignored him, he will probably have received more overt attention and demonstrations of affection than any other member of the household.

He must, therefore, be prepared well in advance for the expected arrival of his sibling. If, indeed, he is over two this is a good opportunity to acquaint him with some of the facts of life: why Mum is getting so big; how Jo can feel the unborn baby kicking, if he puts his hand just here; that it will be either a baby sister or a baby brother, but to start with she will be very small and spend most of her time sleeping. In all these conversations the point should be stressed that Jo II will be a younger sibling *for him*. And it is wise to warn him that he may be unable to see Mum for a day or two: but he'll probably be able to spend more time with Dad – and the latter should in fact be arranged, if possible.

After the birth of Josephine, Jo should get more attention from his parents, rather than less, for a time. He should be encouraged to look at her, to kiss her if he wishes to do so – though not too boisterously. It should be explained to him that she will be able to play with him and talk to him when she is older. It may be inadvisable, however, to leave him alone in the room with Josephine for the first few months. He may, at first, be unable to resist the strong urge to thump her. At some level he is bound to feel that she is ousting him, however carefully he has been prepared and however lovingly his parents treat him after Josephine's arrival.

I recall a close friend of mine who had two daughters, telling me how at three and a half her Joanna said of the baby, born during the war, "Wouldn't it be *lovely* if a bomb fell on Josie!" Such a wish is not uncommon: what was unusual here was the frankness with which

161

Joanna was able to verbalise it, secure in the knowledge that her mother would accept the remark with amused understanding, rather than horror or reproach. These two sisters have been close friends for many decades and have, between them, produced six well-loved children.

Not only should Jo receive extra demonstrativeness from his parents during Josephine's early infancy but they should ensure that friends and guests greet *him* first, before they pay their respects to the baby. This will not distress Josephine who will probably spend most of her time asleep or feeding during the first few weeks – and who, in any case, will accept the family as she finds it. It is desirable, too, to encourage Jo to participate actively in Josephine's programme. Get him to fetch the clean nappy, to find the baby-powder, to test the temperature of the bath-water (though you had better check this as well). Jo will enjoy feeling useful and he may even find interesting all the routine of the baby, and superior that he has grown out of it.

On the other hand, he may well regress to earlier habits as a reaction to Josephine's presence and in a bid to recapture all the attention. If Jo – who had perhaps become dry and clean – takes to wetting or soiling himself; if he – who had walked most of the day – reverts to crawling; or if he becomes a cry-baby ... do not worry unduly. You may simply conclude that he has read the text-books! Do *not*, however, give him extra attention (other than is strictly necessary) in response to these particular ploys, for you do not wish to reinforce them. *Do* give him extra attention and play and smiles when he is being his cheerful pristine self and when he is helping with Josephine – and his regressive phase should soon pass. Jo will then shortly be on his way to the latency period.

Before we discuss this interesting period, however, let us consider the vexed issue of boy/girl differences. Why do we discuss this in the "Two to Five" chapter? And why preface the discussion with the word "vexed"? The first question can be answered more quickly and less controversially than the second. It is indeed arbitrary to consider differences between the sexes at this stage of development rather than in infancy or in adolescence since, if psychological differences do exist, they are likely to be manifested at every age. I choose to do it here, however, because after puberty the differences would seem to be so evident and so important that they would merit a whole book to themselves, and it is not with this topic that the present book is primarily concerned.

162

I am interested in the question whether such differences obtain in toddlers (and even younger) and – if so – whether they can be attributed to nature or nurture. Hence the "vexedness" of the issue. Passions run high in the ranks of Women's Lib at any suggestion that there are psychological differences between little girls and little boys (the existence of physical differences is not, I think, in dispute) *and* that these are innate. Women's Libbers, if I understand them correctly, hold that there are no basic psychological differences between the sexes – i.e. in interests, personality, intelligence or temperament – but that, if any are observed, they are due exclusively to the social environment in which our children are reared.

They seem to hold, too, that "different from" necessarily implies either "superior to" or "inferior to", and that – again in the event of any lurking differences being spotted – the females have the edge on the males. To paraphrase the immortal words of George Orwell: the two sexes are equal but one is more equal than the other.*

My own belief is that, broadly speaking, there are certain differences (and in this instance "broadly speaking" is a meaningful and necessary qualification, to which we return later); and that, in common with all psychological traits, they are due to the combination and interaction of nature and nurture. In general, females of all ages are more interested in people than are males of corresponding ages. This does not render them either superior or inferior but it naturally influences their personality (if this term be interpreted in the sense of the "shop-window" aspect of an individual. For other meanings of the word "personality" see *Intelligence and Personality*).†

As to intelligence, this again seems to be different rather than superior or inferior. In intelligence tests, girls and women score relatively more highly on verbal items, whilst boys and men score relatively more highly on numerical and visuo-spatial items. (Extreme scores – both high and low – are also gained more frequently by males than by females.) These future differences are reflected in play-school – and, some of them, even earlier. Joanna and Josephine tend to talk earlier than Jonathan and Joseph. They do play with child-dolls and tea-sets and model farms, and they enjoy games of nursing and doctoring, to a greater extent. Jonathan and Joseph, on the other hand, are apt to spend more time on toy cars and trains, on Action Man dolls and on mechanical models. Put briefly, and in an over-

*Orwell, George, *Animal Farm*, Chapter 10, p. 87, Secker & Warburg, 1945.
†Heim, Alice, *Intelligence and Personality*, Chapters 6 & 14, Pelican Original, 1970.

simplified way, the typical boy is more interested in what he is doing, whilst the typical girl is more interested in whom she is doing it with. Similar differences may be found in the picture-books most favoured by the boys and by the girls. If we go back a year or two, we find that many baby-girls react pleasurably, even flirtatiously, to men, whether familiar or not, whilst baby-boys – when interested in strangers – tend to pay equal attention to members of both sexes. Many males change in this respect as they grow older!

These are very broad generalisations, hence my insistence on the inclusion of the phrase "broadly speaking" above and my constant use of terms like "tend to" and "typical". Of course some little girls enjoy making models and hammering nails and playing with toy cars; and some little boys talk early and eloquently, and are happiest in highly social play. The generalisations concern the norms – to which there are many exceptions. In my experience, however, they hold even in those homes and play-schools (and the numbers are growing) where members of both sexes are encouraged to choose whatever activities they like – with absolutely no suggestion that trains are not for girls or that dolls are unsuitable for boys.

I have discussed this question with a number of play-school teachers and they – after a respectful, if not a fearful, bow to Women's Lib views and a very relevant admission of their ignorance of parental attitudes to the child at home – tentatively state they are *inclined* to think that there are *probably* boy/girl differences in interests, in *some cases*, and that these *may be* innately rather than socially determined.

For what it is worth, this was the conclusion that I surprisedly reached at home with my two children – with whom I talked and played in the same way from the time they reached me at the respective ages of seven weeks and four weeks. Joanna had, and has retained, "very feminine" interests and outlook; while Jonathan's were always, equally uncompromisingly, "very masculine". My defence for even mentioning such a minute sample is that they were brought up in a household where no playthings were deemed more appropriate for one than the other and in which there was no father-figure for Jonathan to identify with.

I would not deny, however, the powerful effect of such figures (and, equally, of mother figures) in certain families and the pressures for sex-role-playing that are exerted in some sub-cultures. Though strongly in favour of genuinely equal opportunities at all ages, for members of both sexes, I cannot maintain that equal opportunities –

if and when they are achieved – will result in precisely equal gifts and interests. At this stage, I can only comment appreciatively on the humour and aptness of whoever named the relevant law the "Sex-discrimination Act"!

XVIII
Illnesses, Accidents – and Tantrums

Childhood illnesses are far less of a hazard than they used to be, since the advent of immunisation against diphtheria, typhoid, tetanus, polio and measles. Smallpox is thought to have been eradicated throughout the world, and routine vaccination against it, therefore, is no longer recommended. It is unnecessary and the risks of vaccination outweigh the risk of catching the disease.

Jo should, however, still be routinely immunised against the other illnesses mentioned above, both to protect her and to prevent the development of epidemics. Immunisation against measles is now government policy. When going abroad, immunisation against typhoid and cholera is especially important.

The question of immunising Jo against whooping cough is controversial as this has been known to produce damage – in a tiny proportion of cases. It is generally thought that, for most diseases, the dangers of getting the illness far outweigh the possible dangers of immunisation. But since immunisation against whooping cough may be inadvisable for some children, parents should discuss this matter with their doctor.

In healthy children the common infectious diseases like chicken-pox usually affect them less severely than adults. Indeed, this is true also of the somewhat rarer infectious illnesses such as mumps and jaundice. These illnesses can be extremely unpleasant for adults. It is therefore advisable to allow Jo – if otherwise healthy – to be in contact with infectious diseases from nursery school age. (One does not want a babe-in-arms to contract an illness if it can be avoided.) On the other hand, if Jo is going to lead a normal social life, first at play-school and then at ordinary school, she is bound to encounter germs of one kind or another. Thus she will either catch the disease or possess, or

166

develop, a degree of immunity. It is unusual to contract such illnesses a second time and, in the rare instance when this does happen, the attack is liable to be milder than on the first occasion.

My feeling therefore is, "get the almost inevitable diseases young and over with", i.e. between, say, four and fourteen if possible. Parents obviously cannot exactly arrange for this but they can resist the temptation to keep Joanna away from Joseph while he is infectious. Illness never comes at a convenient time: in fact, whenever it strikes, we are inclined to think that it could not have occurred at a worse time! But for various reasons the inconvenience, as well as the severity, tend to increase with age.

It is now well-known that if a woman contracts Rubella (German measles) during the early months of pregnancy, there is risk that the child she is bearing may be born with certain congenital defects. So Joanna should be immunised against this illness before there is any risk of pregnancy. This service is usually offered at about age thirteen.

Apart from infectious diseases such as those mentioned above, young children are prone to catch colds and coughs when they come into daily contact with other children. If they run a temperature and have no other symptoms, they should be kept warm and given plenty of fluids to drink. The temperature of young children will sometimes rise swiftly to an alarming degree, but it can fall again equally quickly. If the temperature persists for more than twenty-four hours or there are any other symptoms, or if you are worried, consult the doctor. Food should not be forced upon children when ill – any more than when they are well – but if they are willing to eat, let them do so. It is not always necessary to keep a sick child in bed if she prefers to be up and has a warm room in which to play.

Occasional indispositions are almost inevitable and, if reasonably mild and infrequent, should not arouse undue anxiety. If, on the other hand, Jo gets a severe sore throat and runs a high temperature every few weeks, sleeps noisily with her mouth open, and the doctor diagnoses this as tonsilitis – then do consider letting her have her tonsils (and adenoids) removed, even if the current fashion is against this; similarly with a persistent tummy ache and a possible "grumbling appendix". Medical fads – like psychological fads – tend to swing from extreme to extreme. In my view, it is as foolish to allow children to suffer from the painful symptoms year after year as it is to whip out their tonsils at the first appearance of a sore throat. If, however, the symptoms repeatedly occur, and your GP is against Jo's being operated on, request a second medical opinion.

Apart from keeping Jo warm, dry and clean, contented and sensibly fed, and giving her plenty of fresh air and exercise, little can be done to keep her free from illness if she is to lead a normal social life. Accidents, however, are another matter: a great many young children sustain accidents, the majority of which could be avoided, given adequate information and care on the part of the parents.

The Health Education Council has published a helpful Guide to Preventing Children's Accidents entitled *Play It Safe!* It opens with the following statistics. On average four children are killed by accidents *every day* [in Britain]. Accidents are the *commonest cause of death* among toddlers and older children. For children between the ages of ten and fifteen, *nearly half* of all deaths are due to accidents. Every year, *one child in every six* goes to a hospital accident and emergency department. *One in every three* of all patients going to a hospital accident and emergency department is a child. *One in every six* children in hospital is there because of an accident (their italics throughout). I am indebted to this Guide for much of the advice given below.

Among the most frequent serious accidents are burns and scalds, drowning, poisoning, road accidents, fractures and concussion due to falls. Let us consider each in turn. It is true that "a burnt child dreads the fire" – but an unburnt child does not! Most heaters look harmless to a child, whether they are radiators, gas fires, electric bar heaters or open fires of the courtier-stove or open grate variety. Indeed, some look positively attractive. All must have guards while Jo is about; and the guards must be effective in practice as well as in theory, i.e. it must not be possible for Jo to pull them over or away from the fire. Most healthy children are curious and active and, once mobile, they will experiment with anything they can.

Another fire-hazard concerns inflammable clothing and inflammable toys. Dress Jo in flame-resistant clothes; and, even then, do not air them by hanging them on the fire-guard. Do not leave Jo alone in a room with a hot iron. It looks deceptively inoffensive. Switch it off as soon as the ironing is finished and keep it, at all times, out of Jo's reach. Boxes of matches and cigarette lighters should be kept out of her reach and out of her sight. If you have any petrol or paraffin, store it in a safe place whither Jo cannot penetrate; beware of old-style paraffin heaters. And remember that Jo may throw things on to the fire, even from her cot.

Scalding can occur through Jo's snatching at your cup of tea or coffee while seated on your knee; through her knocking over – or sampling – a hot drink left on a coffee table or on the floor (a child's skin is far more sensitive than an adult's); or through a toddler's pulling at the flex of an electric kettle, or at the handle of a pan on the cooker, containing boiling-water or oil. It is wise to get in the habit of turning such handles sideways, while they are on the gas jet or electric ring, so that they do not stick out. This sort of habit is advisable even before Jo appears on the scene: one cannot "think of everything" when first having the care of a young child – and, in any case, adults too have been known to bump against an obtruding pan-handle and knock it down, with dire results.

Jo can get scalded also by being bathed in water that is too hot. Always run the cold water into the bath before the hot; do not add hot water while Jo is actually in the bath, and never leave her alone in the bath, even for a few seconds. Children have been known to drown while their mother briefly leaves the bathroom to answer the telephone or the door-bell. If an interruption occurs during Jo's bath-time, lift her out of the bath, wrap her in a towel and take her with you.

Drowning is a serious hazard for young children, largely because it is not generally realised that a toddler can drown in *a few inches* of water. Children love to play with water and they naturally enjoy exploring pools and small ponds and water tanks. At the seaside they like to lie on an inflatable dinghy or lilo – but these can be swept away from the shore and they overturn easily. If Jo wants a go on the lilo, enjoy it with her, whether in the sea or swimming-pool. Constant vigilance is the watchword where water is concerned.

Many households contain medical tablets or liquids which are dangerous if taken in quantity – and which can be lethal if taken by a child. Jo may sample these because they look like sweets, or because she likes to try anything once – or even because she has been expressly forbidden to touch them! The question of forbidding poses a genuine dilemma to parents: that of the matches-up-the-nose problem. In this traditional tale, Mother left the house saying to her children: "Be good; don't let anyone in; and don't put matches up your nose." The last procedure would never have entered the children's heads if it had not been mentioned. But, having heard the suggestion, they not unnaturally tried it! A similar situation may arise with parents who forbid their offspring to sample their medicines. So this fiat is clearly not enough to avert tragedy.

Medicines must be firmly enclosed, preferably in child-resistant containers, and kept in a locked chest or cupboard, with the key in a place unknown to Jo and unattainable by her. Keep an eye on her when she goes on visits – especially to the elderly, who may be taking tablets regularly and whose house may not be geared to young children.

Medicines are not, of course, the only poisons to be found in a contemporary household. Bleach, furniture-polish, lavatory-cleaner, ammonia, disinfectants and many other useful products may be available – including designated poisons such as rat-poison and weed-killer. Never store such things in a harmless-looking bottle, and always label them clearly. Risk of poisoning is not confined to the house. Certain plants and fungi may be swallowed by the enterprising child on a country walk, and some of them may cause violent indigestion (such as laburnum seeds or lords-and-ladies), while others, such as certain toadstools, can actually kill.

Even toys have their dangers. Make sure that the paint on Jo's toys is safe – and, preferably, that it will not come off if licked or handled with sticky fingers. Toys that come to pieces (if not so intended) can be dangerous: a teddy-bear's eye or a small doll's hand, once detached, is likely to find its way into young Jo's mouth – and, hence, into her throat or stomach. Toys with sharp edges can cut. Try to give her toys that are safe even when old, and when not used as they were designed to be used. If they do start disintegrating they should either be mended or thrown away.

At toddler-age and later, Jo may enjoy drawing and scribbling, and cutting-out. Never let her run around with a pencil in her mouth, and make sure that her cutting-out scissors have rounded ends – but also that they *can* cut paper! Some children become so frustrated by their blunt scissors that they rummage in Mum's sewing basket, where they may encounter needles and pins as well as sharp, pointed scissors. They may also find needles and pins stuck into the arms of a stuffed sofa or arm-chair, if Mum uses these as a pin-cushion. This is a habit that it is wise to drop before Jo is even thought of!

Road accidents are among the most frequent and serious of mishaps. If young children are not hand-held or on walking reins, they are likely to sustain a road accident. You will of course teach Jo from early years to keep to the pavement in town; to cross at pedestrian crossings; and, always, to listen and to look both ways before crossing the road. But such behaviour does not become automatic for many years (in some cases, never!)

It must be remembered that, even if Jo has learned the correct procedure, until she is about ten years old her judgment of car-speed and of distance will not match that of an adult (who has taken years to acquire the skill). Apart from accidents due to this misperception, others are very likely to happen if Jo is playing with a ball in the street: she will naturally dart after it if it bounces into the road. Ball-games of any kind should be banned in the street.

Parked vehicles are a special hazard: neither the fast-moving child nor the car-driver can see through them and both are apt to forget the existence of the other. Drivers should *expect* all children to move quickly and thoughtlessly – as, indeed, they should expect foolish behaviour from other drivers. They should anticipate the little group hidden by the ice-cream van and the temptation of the children to play "last one across". But, as a rule, drivers don't. It is therefore up to parents to anticipate on behalf of Jo; to train her and rehearse her, to ensure that she is not allowed in the street alone before she can cope; and to realise that Jo, out of parents' sight and with a group of playmates, may behave very differently from Jo-with-parent.

Most children fall down now and then. They do like to run before they can walk, their sense of balance takes a while to develop and, as suggested in Chapter XVII, a fall to the floor will probably do no harm. In this chapter, however, we are concerned with more serious falls resulting, perhaps, in concussion or a fracture: a fall from a window or balcony, or from a swiftly moving swing, a fall on to concrete from a tall climbing-frame or a fall down a flight of stairs. Let us consider the last example first.

Until Jo has learned to go up and down stairs on her own, it is best to use a safety-gate, at top and bottom of the stairs. But she will see unprotected staircases in other houses and will make a beeline for them if given the chance. She must be taught *to go downstairs backwards*. She will probably manage surprisingly well to climb the stairs from the age of a year or less; but at the top she must learn to turn herself round and clamber down with her chest to the stairs. This is much safer than walking downstairs, or than bumping downstairs on her bottom. It is also useful training for coming down ladders and trees when older and – if she should take to rock-climbing – for a mountaineering descent. Jo will take pleasure in learning to turn herself round at the top of the staircase and, once she has acquired the skill, she will enjoy the freedom of the stairs. This will, of course, take time and patience.

If a baby has a fall before she can crawl or walk, this is emphatically the parent's fault. An infant should never be left lying on a bed, for instance: she may easily roll off it. Nor should she be left in a bouncing-chair or cradle, on a table: she may bounce the whole bouncer off the table. The harness should always be fastened, whether on a bouncing-cradle, high-chair, pram or push-chair.

Beware of locks and bolts on doors at Jo-height. For some reason it is usually easier for a child to lock herself in than to let herself out. To find oneself locked in lavatory or bathroom can produce panic. Beware too of electric plugs and gas-taps; of giving Jo boiled sweets or nuts – particularly peanuts, which can become stuck in the wind-pipe – until she has a well-developed set of teeth; and of fire-arms, including pop-guns and air-pistols. And beware of the ubiquitous plastic bag: it may appeal to Jo as a toy but if she places it over her head, she may suffocate.

Once a child is mobile there are two main principles to observe. Do give training and help (as in road-drill and descending the stairs) while not destroying the child's self-confidence. And do make sure that Jo is never left alone in any potentially dangerous situation – and that means pretty well every situation!

This chapter ends with a note on tantrums. These are, of course, neither illnesses nor accidents – though, in extreme cases, they may lead to one or the other. A tantrum consists of violent, uncontrolled screaming, with or without tears, and usually vigorous movements of the whole body – but sometimes Jo may elect to lie down (on floor or earth) to kick and scream. "Uncontrolled" it is, at the beginning, but it may well become uncontrollable, that is, Jo may continue to yell and fight when she no longer "wishes" to do so and after she has forgotten the initial cause of the trouble. In prolonged cases it may even develop into hysterics or a kind of fit.

Tantrums are distressing and worrying for Jo's parents and, indeed, for anyone else who may be within earshot; they are shame-making in public places such as shops and parks; and they are bad for Jo, both physically and psychologically. If a child is given to attacks of uncontrollable rage in infancy, these are liable to continue into childhood and perhaps even later. Most children are quite capable of producing tantrums and, in my view, they should not be allowed to occur – and need never have occurred, if evasive action be taken early enough.

A tantrum arises, typically, if a child who has been spoilt (that is, always given her own way and persistently allowed to ignore directions) is crossed: either denied what she wants when she wants it, or if an attempt is made to get her to do something she does not wish to do. In such circumstances, brief wailing or crying is unsurprising: such behaviour should not be "rewarded", however, by a change of mind on the parent's part. If Jo's plaint continues after a firm NO, it is

172

best ignored. Do not punish her and do not leave her by herself, but turn your back on her and, if others are present, talk to them quietly – about anything except Jo! A tantrum is unlikely to develop if the child fails to gain attention by it; and, if attention is lost early on, the uncontrollable stage will probably never be reached.

Many parents faced with a vociferous young child will either scold or smack her or, after a while, give in. Sometimes both these reactions are evoked consecutively. Once Jo learns that if she makes enough fuss for a sufficiently long time she will prevail, she will very naturally "create" more and more loudly and violently. Thus is born the habit of throwing tantrums. They will not only exhaust her and drain her parents' energy: the tantrums may occasionally do Jo some harm – for instance, if she is ill and should not become over-excited. So, at such times, do not give Jo extra attention (whether appeasing or irate) – rather, withdraw it temporarily. (Interestingly enough, *Longman's Modern English Dictionary* actually defines TANTRUM as "a fit of bad temper indulged in *before another person or persons*" [my italics]. This would seem to confirm my suggestion of the efficacy of inattention.) Once Jo has recovered, however, do demonstrate your love and affection, after a pause. If you hasten to make too much of her as soon as peace is regained, the whole affair may start again!

I have met some parents who take the line that they should at all costs "avoid confrontation". But I believe this to be mistaken. It is crucial for Jo to learn to tolerate frustration and to learn also that a conflict with parents does not denote any withdrawal of affection. For this to be learnt, there must be occasional overt conflict.

When Jo grows angry because she wants the bright star on top of the Christmas tree or because she is prevented from tearing wallpaper off the wall, I do not think it a good idea always to divert her: to sweep her up into your arms, for instance, saying, "Look at the pretty lights over here," or, "Come and have a piggy-back ride" . . . Once she has accepted that some things are unattainable or forbidden, life will become *less* frustrating for her and she may be allowed greater freedom. When the point at issue is Jo's wish to continue some pleasurable activity that must be brought to a close, a compromise can often be effected by means of the 1, 2, 3 method, described in Chapter XV.

173

XIX
The Latency Period

The term "latency period" was originally coined by the psychoanalysts to refer to the period between four–five years of age and about twelve years of age. They used the term especially in relation to the development of the individual's sexuality. Thus they considered four–five to mark the end of "infantile sexuality" and to herald the approach of a few years of relative tranquillity, without the *Sturm und Drang* that accompanies the onset of puberty, usually at eleven–thirteen.

I am critical of a good deal of psychoanalytic theory and practice: for instance, the fact that none of its tenets can be disproved (indeed it must be one of the few doctrines, outside religion, in which *whatever* occurs is taken by its adherents as confirmation of its truth); the tendency to "interpret" the spoken word as though saying what one actually means is virtually impossible – and as though one and only one interpretation of what is said (namely, that of the current interpreter) is correct; the implication, eagerly inferred by many, that nothing unpleasant that happens to us is ever our own fault; and the exaggerated emphasis on sexuality – absurdly *under*-stressed though this was before Freud.

I believe, however, that psychoanalysis performed an exceedingly useful function in its exposé of much that was (and still is) hypocritical in our behaviour and speech; and in prompting us to rethink a great many of our hitherto accepted conventions, idioms – and modes of bringing up children.

I find, too, that the concept of a latency period between pre-school age and adolescence is valuable, and that there is no other phrase that so well characterises that time of life. Hence my adoption of the term for the title of this chapter. It is tempting to say that this period of the child's life is a particularly interesting one for the parent, but – as most people will agree who have shared an individual's development with him from infancy to adulthood – every period has its own particular interest.

During the first weeks of babyhood, parents are constantly exclaiming, "I had no idea they could be such fun at this early age! . . . He's beginning to smile already – no, that wasn't wind . . . He can actually recognise us . . . He holds up his head now . . ." and so it continues. Again, Jo is enchanting as a toddler, enjoying his new-found mobility and relative independence. During his teens, his parents may bewail the problems and the rebellions, but they cannot claim that Jo's developing personality lacks interest. And finally, when Jo comes of age – legally, emotionally, intellectually – this is tremendously exciting.

Why, then, do I suggest that the latency period is of special interest? Perhaps because it is the time, if all has gone well with Jo, when he begins to realise his own individuality, almost consciously. I say " if all has gone well", because if Jo has experienced a number of different parents or foster-homes, or if his biological parents have separated, such traumata may delay or impair the dawning of self-identity.

All being well, however, the latency period is a pleasantly relaxing time for Jo and his parents, a time to sit back and take stock. The child has now acquired a useful working vocabulary: he can express what he wants to convey (see Chapter XXI for examples). This may mean voicing disagreements; or delightedly learning a new idea via a new word (or conversely); or – challengingly, if sometimes irritatingly – asking WHY? Let me give some illustrations of these.

One of my happiest and most amusing recollections of long ago concerns an unknown child of about four, whom I passed in the street, holding his mother's hand and evidently involved in angry altercation. As I walked past – sporting a brightly coloured pair of trousers (not so commonly worn by women at that time), hair blown on end by the breeze and swinging a squash racquet – I heard the four-year-old saying furiously to his mother, "But I don't *want* to see the funny lady!" Had he been a year or two younger, he would probably just have turned his head away, thus affording less entertainment to me and, no doubt, to his companion.

Learning a new word or a new concept can give a young child inordinate pleasure – which, of course, communicates itself to his parents. I remember, when my Jo was about five, we were scribbling

175

and doodling together and we both drew a three-sided figure (of very different shape), whereupon I said, "That's a triangle – and *that's* a triangle." Jo repeated the word without marked enthusiasm. A few days later, however, we went out to tea with an old lady who had a small three-sided patch of grass immediately outside her front door. Jo took one look at this and shouted, "It's a triangle! It's a TRIANGLE!" delighted to recognise it, to name it and to inform everybody within hearing. On another occasion, we were walking up river on a gloriously sunny day, hoping to find a free punt – but all seemed to be occupied and moving – when Jo suddenly exclaimed triumphantly, "There's a STATIONARY punt!" having heard the word a day or two earlier. And again, at five or six, when the sun came out and he saw his shadow appear, he exclaimed, "Look, there's a REFLECTION on the pavement!"

The acquisition of new words determines the acquisition of new concepts, and conversely. Not all children have strong verbal interests, however, just as adults vary in this respect. Some children are keener on physically constructive activities such as building model aircraft or taking clocks to pieces, preparatory – sometimes – to re-assembling them; others enjoy more domestic pursuits, such as organising mini-tea-parties or learning to carve the joint; while yet others prefer drawing and painting; and some children take great pleasure in ball-games – throwing, catching and kicking a ball.

The mastery of words, however, is an enjoyable phenomenon, in that it enables Jo to express his feelings, to crystallise his ideas, to communicate with others: this is a two-way process and it imbues the young speaker with an impression of power that implicitly increases his self-confidence. The child may not realise this at the time, but the frustration and *lack* of confidence in a child who has difficulties with speech are abundantly clear.

Such difficulties may arise because Jo's interests lie in more manual or visual realms, because he is partially deaf or has a tongue- or mouth-defect; or – and this is of primary concern to us here – because he has not received sufficient verbal stimulation from his companion, probably his mother or baby-minder. As we have seen in Chapter XII, it is vital *to talk* to a baby from birth onwards. If the parents acquire this habit in early days, it is easy and natural to continue, and talking to Jo becomes increasingly rewarding as he grows older.

These joys, however, are accompanied by certain other develop-ments that not all parents find pleasing, in particular negativism and questioning. "I don't *want* to see the funny lady" is an excellent example of negativism. Jo has learned to say NO! long before he reaches the latency period, but it is usually only after the age of four or five that he elaborates on his denials. Similarly with questioning and, in particular, the question WHY? Some Why-questions are answerable and others are not. I think it highly desirable to reply to those that are answerable, and to answer them honestly and rationally – even if this sometimes means saying, "I don't know, but I'll find out." "Because I say so" may be an honest reply but it is not a very rational one, in Jo's opinion. If you have said that he is not to sit in the front of the car or is not to play in the garden today or is not to suck his bus ticket . . . you presumably have your reasons and it is advisable to inform Jo of them. Imposing this discipline on oneself, incidentally, sometimes reveals that one did not have very good reasons: one up to Jo!

On the other hand some Why-questions are meaningless and as such are best ignored. In this way Jo will soon learn not to overwork this potent weapon. Ignoring is especially effective in this situation, for the asking of Why-questions that are meaningless is more often a bid for attention than a request for information.

Bidding for attention may be just a habit – which Jo should have grown out of before he reaches the latency period. But sometimes it stems from boredom, for instance during a long journey in a car or train. It is well to be prepared with books and puzzles for such eventualities. Those puzzles that involve shifting letters or numbers around to make a given pattern or sequence (e.g., alphabetical or odd or even numbers grouped together) are useful, for they are small, light and unbreakable, and they appeal to many children. There are also the more sociable games, such as "I spy . . .", "I love my love with an A", and "My grandmother went to Paris", which require collaboration from the adults.

A friend of mine devised a game called Silly-billy Motorist for use with his two sons, on car journeys. He describes it as follows: "The child scores, against another child, the parent, or simply in the abstract, different points from 1–5 for any observed breach of the Highway Code, e.g. 5 for an actual accident caused, 4 for overtaking before – or on – the crest of a hill, etc. My boys often scored 1 by observing that *I* was driving at more than thirty miles per hour in a built-up area. Very educative game!" The chance of indicting Dad would certainly add spice to the game, from the child's point of view. And, as the deviser comments, it is highly educational – for both generations – and the game probably stood his sons in good stead when they, themselves, became car-drivers. Make the most of this period when parent co-operation is enjoyed for, in a few short years, it may no longer be sought – or even accepted, if offered!

This is also a good time for games-playing at home, with family and friends: card games, such as Snap, Beggar-my-Neighbour, Happy Families – leading on to Rummy and, perhaps, Whist and Bridge; "acting" games, such as Charades (many kinds), Adverbs, Proverbs; boisterous games, such as Blind Man's Buff, Hunt the Slipper, Musical Bumps; paper-and-pencil games, such as Consequences, Noughts and Crosses, Heads-bodies-and-tails, Boxes; board games, such as Snakes and Ladders, Nine Men's Morris, Draughts and Chess (for two), Ludo and Halma (for two to four), Monopoly and Bingo for almost any number.

Most children enjoy these once they have got the hang of them: they must not be frightened off them at the beginning. Such games are not ostensibly instructive (a feature which does antagonise many children) yet they have educational value in two respects. First, they demand recognition of numbers or letters or other symbols, or swift reactions, or learning to look ahead. Secondly, many of these games end with a winner – and, hence, with one or more losers. Jo has to learn the important lesson of losing gracefully. This lesson, ironically enough, is hardest for the players who are keen and good at the game (partly, perhaps, because they have less practice at losing!). Young people of today have the excellent object-lesson of top tennis player, John McEnroe: no one can doubt his keenness and skill, nor can one doubt that he failed to learn in childhood the art of losing gracefully.

During Jo's first few years at school, two of the topics that are liable to crop up are pocket-money and religion. Jo will soon become aware that the majority of his schoolfellows are receiving weekly pocket-money and if you do not broach the matter, he will probably do so. It is a good plan to discuss it jointly with Jo and your spouse. Try to find out the going rate – the highest and the lowest amounts that Jo's schoolmates are getting – and, in my opinion, it will be best for Jo if he receives a weekly pay-packet towards the middle of the range. This should be paid regularly, without prompting and given as a right, not as a favour.

He should receive pocket-money partly because it is "only fair" that he should enjoy the same privileges as other boys and girls and also because this is how he will eventually learn to manage his own financial affairs. One cannot learn to use or to save money if one does not possess any. Furthermore, the time is coming – or it may already have arrived – when Jo wants to give his parents and friends presents for Christmas and birthdays. He may elect to construct these gifts, himself, but even so he will need to come by the materials.

I have no doubts about the correctness of paying Jo weekly pocket-money. The question of religion, however, is much more difficult. Almost all schools pay lip-service to prayers and "religious education": some take it a great deal more seriously than that. If Jo's parents are themselves religious and his school offers the same type of religion as they profess – whether Protestantism, Catholicism, Judaism, Buddhism, etc. – there is no problem and no confusion for Jo at this stage. His two life-contexts confirm one another. If the attitudes differ, however, or if the parents are humanists, agnostics or atheists, then a decision must be taken to avoid Jo's becoming bewildered and worried, about a matter that he realises pervades the whole essence of life for many.

In such circumstances, Jo's parents should, I think, maintain their habitual sincerity and straightforwardness with him. But he is not yet old enough to be able to assimilate conflicting basic attitudes. So it is unwise to dismiss the school's teaching in this sphere as mistaken or speculative. Listen with interest to what Jo passes on and, if he questions you about its verity or about your own views, tell him – as is indeed the case – that different people have different ideas and everybody is entitled to their own view.

If Jo should ask his humanist parents, for instance, for a prayer to say at night, suggest a short child's prayer or help him to make one up. A conflict on these matters may put a great strain on him during his first years at school. There will be plenty of time for theological discussion when Jo is reaching the end of the latency period – and then he is quite likely to reopen the question himself.

Five to twelve is a period during which new friendships are formed – sometimes destined to last a lifetime, but sometimes lasting only a few weeks, or less. Encourage the making of friends by welcoming them if Jo wishes to bring them home and by allowing Jo to visit them if he so desires. He may like to have a friend to stay over half-term, or for a few days during a vacation. Do not overtly disapprove of them, even if you feel that some are ill-chosen. Jo will realise that you like some of his friends less than others and he is more likely to take note of the fact if you make no comment. Do not ask too many questions of his guests, but *do* help them to leave when the time is ripe! Briskly rising to one's feet and moving towards the door saying, "Well it's been good to see you," will work wonders. At this stage children sometimes find it difficult to initiate their departure, even when they wish to do so (and, in time to come, you may find the technique of inoffensively speeding the static guest to be useful even with older people). Jo's friends may also appreciate being told where the lavatory is, for they are often too shy to ask. It is a good idea to train Jo to convey this information himself.

During the latency period, many boys and girls like to join organised groups, such as Cubs and Brownies, or camping or swimming clubs. There is evidently a pleasant feeling of *belonging* with some others of roughly the same age, coupled with a feeling of independence since these groups are not closely associated with home or, necessarily, with school. At this stage many children prefer to spend most of their spare time with others of their own sex, though – as with all such generalisations – there are exceptions to this.

Most English children have not learned to swim by the time they are five years old, unlike young children in warmer climates. Whether or not Jonathan or Joanna like water, it is vital that they know how to swim, preferably by the time they are six. Indeed, if they dislike or fear the water it is even more important that they should learn. On the positive side, feeling at home in the water is highly enjoyable, and this enjoyment is unattainable until one feels happy out of one's depth and able to trust the water. Moreover, swimming is a skill that inspires a confidence extending beyond the swimming-pool and the sea. On the negative side, the non-swimmer is at risk – and acutely aware of being at risk – in many situations. In addition to the possibility of drowning, such risks include non-participation in certain social events and probable teasing by schoolmates, or even teachers. Moreover, with increasing years comes increasing difficulty: postponing the problem is as self-defeating as postponing a visit to the dentist when one has toothache.

For a child with a water-phobia the choice of swimming-teacher is crucial. But whether Jo's father or mother decides to take it on, or whether they invoke a friend or a professional teacher, it should be someone patient and gentle, who understands the nature of a phobia. The old notion of "chucking him in at the deep end" has nothing to be said for it. Far from achieving its object, it may leave Jo with an abiding hatred and fear of water (and of the chucker) – and an inability to swim.

Swimming has a further virtue, related to a very different stage from the latency period, namely, to Jo's middle age and old age. Like most skills, once learnt it is never forgotten. And swimming – unlike competititve sports such as squash and football – is not only possible, but actively good, for older people: it has therapeutic value in that one can exercise muscles without undue effort and without having to bear one's weight, since the water bears it. But, again like most skills, it is infinitely harder to learn when old than when young.

These considerations apply also to other activities that are practical and enjoyable. Jo will be delighted if you get him a bicycle and teach him to ride when he is between five and twelve. Bicycles for young children, with stabilising wheels, are available and the additional little wheels can be removed once Jo has gained his balance. He will be eager to go on to this next stage. It is a good idea to teach him also the rudiments of puncture-repairing and bicycle-maintenance if he is willing and you are competent.

The specifically social skills are more difficult to instil (though example may play a part) but they are extremely important for, if Jo gets on well with strangers and makes friends easily, this will prove an asset to him throughout life. One way of affording practice in social intercourse at a superficial level is to get Jo to do some shopping with you – if you can find any small shops such as still exist in villages, as opposed to the impersonal supermarket type of store. Let him learn the virtue of prefacing his request with a "good morning" or "good afternoon", of explaining just what he wishes to purchase, and of checking the change.

This is especially useful practice for Jo if he is inclined to be shy or self-conscious. If he is allowed to add the occasional bar or chocolate or packet of sweets or crisps to his shopping-list, this should assist him to overcome his initial timidity. Some children grow positively to enjoy shopping, but those who do not will at least be able to cope without difficulty when, at a later stage, they need to be able to shop on their own.

Two further activities worth considering are self-defence and playing a musical instrument. If Jo goes to classes in Judo (or one of the other self-defending sports), the art may prove valuable in later life – and perhaps even more valuable to Joanna than to Jonathan. It inspires confidence in oneself and respect from peers; again, it involves learning how to fall; and, once learnt, the body always remembers it.

Arranging for Jo to take music lessons is more controversial. Many parents hold that if Jo is really musical, this will become apparent and he will ask to have lessons in, say, piano-playing. Both suppositions are dubious. Jo may not sing in tune at five or six (or later) but he may have a strong sense of rhythm – which is one of the main essentials for key-board instruments (and, of course, percussion). Indeed he may even have a good ear for pitch but lack the ability to produce the sound he hears in his head. He is, in fact, unlikely to request music lessons, unless he is exceptionally musical; and, even if he does start having lessons, he is extremely unlikely to enjoy practising, unless he has an imaginative teacher who understands young children, and a parent who is willing to practise good-humouredly with him.

"Is it worth the hassle, then?" ask one's friends, observing the squabbles, the mutual resentment and the bargaining, "Just five more minutes then – not a second longer!" I think it *is* worth the hassle, largely because so many of my contemporaries have said to me, "If only they had made me go on after the first year!" Some adults who feel this do embark on lessons, but it is certainly harder to make progress when you are forty or sixty than when you are six or eight, despite the stronger motivation. (The same holds for learning languages.)

My other reasons are that even rebellious young pupils enjoy playing their pieces to guests at home and taking part in school concerts; they grow to understand the basic language of music and learn to listen with pleasure; and a fair proportion of them joyfully continue to play in adulthood. Moreover if their first instrument is the piano, they learn to co-ordinate hand, eye and foot, and to dissociate the movements of one hand from those of the other, and the latter is beneficial in other ways (such as learning to type and to drive). If Jo or his teacher repeatedly and bitterly plead for secession, it is best not to force the issue. Recorder-playing can also provide a good entry to music. It is taught in a number of schools as part of the normal syllabus and it is less demanding than the piano or a stringed instrument.

Music is not of course the only art which may give Jo pleasure. He may enjoy drawing, painting, modelling. Indeed, he may like these from the start as they are more rewarding than are most musical instruments in the early stages. If Jo does manifest interest in the visual arts, give him every encouragement, both material and mental, and consider letting him have extra lessons, in or out of school. Carpentry is another possibility – with aesthetic as well as useful aspects – for both sexes.

Finally, try to inculcate in Jo the habit of reading for pleasure. This is more difficult than it used to be, with the prevalence of television

and the scorn with which many of his peers will treat literature. Offer
him books that will interest him (as opposed to books you think he
ought to read), take him to the local library, and discuss with him
books that he has read. Don't push it too hard and do take the line that
any reading is better than none.

XX

The Facts of Life

My father informed me that he had made this trip especially to have a talk with me; "I understand from your mother that you are considering getting married."

"Well, I was," I said, "But –"

He interrupted. "So I think it's the right moment to have a talk to you about the physical side of any possible relationship. For instance, you see that boy and girl across the other side of the pier – well you see, that is what one could call magnetism. In other words, they are, in a way . . . er . . . attracted to each other, rather like the north and south poles."

"I see," I said.

"You see, it really is a question of nature. That's what it is, nature I mean . . . shall we say . . . fertilization. Take for instance a . . . bee."

"Where to?" I said.

He didn't see the joke, and pressed on. "Well, I mean, in an orchard. There's a male tree and a female tree, and, mmm . . . they need bees to fertilize or pollinate," he said. "And of course it's the same with that boy and girl sitting on the bench. So you see it's really quite simple. And I'm sure . . . very easy to understand. So I don't really think you'll have very much of a problem. Would you like a beer?"

We went to the local pub together, and I could see that he was enormously relieved; he had done his duty as a father.

(Excerpt from the autobiography of Sir John Mills,
Up in the Clouds, Gentlemen Please)

It is worth noting that this conversation took place in 1926, when John Mills was eighteen years of age; and that, at about seven, he had received more explicit instruction from twins of his own generation, his only reaction having been, "But you don't mean the King and Queen do it?" There are perhaps still funnier instances of parents battling bravely, but the above example serves my purpose in that it is

184

typical of the quandary in which parents sometimes find themselves and it illustrates their occasional total failure of communication.

The phrase "facts of life" connotes the facts of sexual intercourse, conception, birth and puberty. Despite the Permissive Society and the increasing frequency of sex education in schools, some young people grow up uninformed or misinformed on these matters. Sex is still regarded by many of them as mysterious and slightly smutty. This is not surprising in view of the attitude of some educationists and some parents. For example, those schools that have instituted sex education classes usually ask permission of the parents to allow their child to attend the course. This request is unlikely to be made for any other courses; and, in all probability, those parents who refuse to give their consent are precisely those whose sons and daughters would most benefit from sexual enlightenment.

The school which my daughter Joanna attended from the age of seven to seventeen, was one of the earliest in the field. The course consisted of four lecture-discussions for the girls age eleven–twelve years, preceded by an excellent introductory discussion with the parents. The talks were given by a mother-of-four biologist, Mrs Berberis, who had charm and humour. After the four classes, the school organised an evening session for the relevant parents to meet again and exchange views on the success of the course. I well recall (though it was some fifteen years ago) how in the middle of this meeting one mother rose to her feet, quivering with rage and embarrassment. "We *never* talk of sex at home," she alleged, wholly convincingly, her voice high and shaking, "We'd never *dream* of doing so – and I think the whole thing is quite unnecessary." In the uneasy silence that followed, some of us sat mulling over the felicitous ambiguity of Mrs Nightshade's proclamation.

That particular course was deemed a success by most parents because our daughters enjoyed it and they certainly learned something from it. Apart from the information – both biological and social – that was conveyed, the mere fact of bringing the matter out into the open and the welcoming of public discussion was salutary. Moreover, it enabled the girls to discuss it among themselves in a more knowledge-able and less furtive manner than hitherto. Anxieties were lessened and many felt that a sharing of the more emotive aspects of sex was now possible – in some cases with members of the older generation.

I believe, however, that eleven–twelve is too old for the first revelations and that the earliest intimations should come from the parents. Many parents would agree in theory with both these

185

statements, but in the event they do not do the job – because "the right moment never presents itself", or "my husband/wife would do it better", or "the child has never enquired" . . . In a word, some parents find it too embarrassing; hence they find that they have procrastinated – until they relievedly assume that the need for such a talk is past. In my experience it is quite untrue that Jo will ask "as soon as (s)he is ready". Some children do so, but in the kind of household which implicitly encourages such an enquiry they will probably have come across related topics gradually and matter-of-factly from an early age.

This was what I endeavoured to achieve with my Joanna and Jonathan. It is doubly important in the case of adopted children, since the earlier they grasp the meaning of the word "adoption" the less traumatic it is for them, and the meaning is of course intrinsically bound up with the facts of life. When the adopter is single, the matter is perhaps trebly important!

My two were used to being introduced as "my adopted children" from their earliest infancy but when they were, respectively, four and three years old, they had not asked me what "adopted" meant nor had they shown any interest in how they were born. (Joanna had spent a weekend with an ex-Nanny and her parents, who bred pigs, and it was related to me how on the Sunday morning they took her to see the litter of baby piglets – not present on the Saturday evening. "Where did they *come* from?" asked Joanna. "So you explained?" I enquired delightedly, of ex-Nanny's Mum. "Oh, I said the fairies had brought them," said the Mum, smiling understandingly at me, "I didn't think you'd like . . ." her voice tailed off).

Shortly after this I read a very favourable review of a book called *Peter and Caroline*, described as an account of the facts of life for four–eight-year-olds. I bought it and read it and placed it among the other books on the low book-shelf from which my children used to choose their evening reading. I read them a story every evening after their bath – the book being chosen by Joanna on Mondays, Wednesdays and Fridays and by Jonathan on Tuesdays, Thursdays and Saturdays. It was many months before this book was selected. The children were by this time five and four and, as I read it to them and showed them the pictures, I gained the impression that they were uninterested and abstracted. Joanna was wriggling her toes and twisting the sash of her dressing-gown in a way that suggested boredom – not embarrassment – and Jonathan was gazing up at the ceiling. When I reached the end, they made no comment.

186

Next day at lunch, however, four-year-old Jonathan suddenly said, "It was *fun* when I was in your tummy, Mummy." I drew a deep breath and said, "Well, you weren't actually in mine, darling, because I adopted you –" at which he looked downcast and quite shocked. I hastened on: "But of course you were in *somebody's* tummy because that's how everyone is born." Needless to say, he found no consolation in this, and he was silent and thoughtful throughout the remainder of the meal. It was a sad moment of truth for both of us but it was now clear that he knew what adoption meant and that he would never have to re-live that particular pang. A few hours later I overheard him telling his teddy-bear, of which he was very fond, "Some grow in their Mummy's tummy and some don't."

Joanna made no comment at the time and it was only when, at seven and a half, she came back from school, radiantly bursting with news that I was certain she knew. "Rosalie's adopted too!" she cried, beaming. "Can we have her to tea on Saturday?"

Awareness of sex-differences and what follows from them can start in babyhood and, in my view, it is highly desirable to encourage this. For instance, if you have two young children, bath them together. If they are of the opposite sex, so much the better: they will notice the differences whether or not they comment on them. I remember Joanna, aged about two and a half, commenting on Jonathan's genitals. "Yes," I said, "that's called his 'penis'." "I haven't got one," said Joanna. "No, because you're a girl. But you'll have breasts, when you're older – like these" (demonstrating the bulge in my pullover). "Shan't I get breasts?" asked Jonathan . . . and so the conversation flowed.

If you do not have two children or you have two of the same sex, the opportunity may come equally naturally at nursery school. These schools usually have a row of little open lavatories; and I recall being told how a small girl – watching a small boy standing and urinating – remarked, "What a handy little thing!"

Not only did I bath my two together and let them share a bedroom until they were about eight and nine years of age, I also encouraged them to visit me in the bathroom, to share my bed for some minutes on Sunday mornings, and to come and talk to me when I was dressing or undressing. Although not a "naturist" I see nothing shameful or offensive in nudity; and I believed that taking this line might lessen some of the problems that beset adolescents, and even some adults, who have never seen a naked body belonging to a member of the opposite sex and who have not had the opportunity to discuss bodily

187

matters, freely and naturally, with someone of the older generation.

This approach worked out as I had hoped. The following conversations (recorded by me within the week) give some idea of the openness and intimacy so engendered. Joanna, aged six, in bed with me, cheek to cheek one Sunday morning, suddenly said affectionately: "You've got such a lovely furry cheek, Mummy!" And when Jonathan aged five was bathing me one day, he said – while washing my breasts – "You fed me with these, didn't you?" I explained why I had not been able to do so. He then asked why I was not married. I replied that nobody I cared for enough had asked me and that now I did not really want to get married. Jonathan said vigorously that that was very silly, that everybody ought to get married and he then suggested Hilary Ilex (a frequent visitor, greatly liked by him and his sister). I said, "He's at least fifteen years younger than I am, to start with." Jonathan: "Oh, you have to be the same age, do you?"

Some minutes later the conversation went as follows. Jon: "You're nearly finished." Mother: "Yes, there's just my legs and my bottom. Which will you do?" Jon: "Your legs" – pause – then, surveying my pubes, "Rather a lot of hair there, isn't there?" M: "Yes, you'll probably have hair there when you're older; and Joanna will have, when she's a woman, just like this." Jon: "You don't cut it here? . . . Only under the arms?" I found this interesting, as I had never discussed or demonstrated the depilating of armpits.

A child brought up in this way does not develop the furtive-cum-knowing attitude to bodily functions that many teenagers go through. They have no need to be aggressively "knowing" as they do indeed know what it is all about. They grow up neither prudish nor prurient. Nor, I may add, do they grow up lacking in modesty or *pudeur*. I observed, fascinated, how first Joanna at about twelve – and, later, Jonathan at much the same age – began knocking at the door when I was bathing or dressing (which they had not done in the past); and how, shortly after this, they ceased to visit me at such times. They also made it clear that they wished their own privacy to be respected. Different as they are from each other in temperament and personality, they both reacted in this way; and (now both married) neither of them went through a sexually promiscuous stage.

Another fact of life – for many, still a taboo topic – is, paradoxically, the fact of death. Many adults lower their voice when speaking of death to contemporaries and they may maintain a strict silence on the subject when in the presence of children. This seems to me not only unnecessary but a positive mistake from the viewpoint of Jo's well-being. We all have to come to terms with death sooner or later, regarding both our own eventual demise and that of those whom we love – although some of us seem to postpone acceptance of our own mortality until the latest possible moment! Most children are resilient, adaptable and realistic. They understand the irrevocability of death – in the sense that it happens to us all and that, once it happens, there is no going back – provided that their parents take a commonsensical line. By that I mean that they neither ignore it nor harp on it nor play down the grief that may be felt by survivors.

A few weeks after the death of our well-loved fourteen-year-old dog, Robin, Joanna, aged nearly five, suddenly remarked to me, "When you're dead, there'll be no more Mummy." She did not say it sadly or smilingly, but very thoughtfully – presumably inspired by Robin's recent death. I was glad that she had achieved this realisation and delighted that she felt able to verbalise it to me. Despite her upbringing, it is likely that she would have censored the remark a few years later.

The loss of a person or an animal dear to one is of course a devastating experience, whenever it happens. But such experience is part of the patchwork of living; and if children are sheltered from such experience it leaves them more vulnerable – not less – and it also diminishes their capacity for empathising with the bereavements of others.

So the message of this chapter is that parents should take the responsibility of instructing their sons and daughters on the basics of life just as seriously as they take their eating habits and their physical health. Some "primitive people", with their various initiation rites, set great store by such instruction. Whilst we may not wish to employ the same techniques, we might well learn from them a useful lesson in priorities.

A list of books written (a) for boys and girls to read and (b) for parents who seek guidance in introducing their children to the facts of life, is given at the end of this book.

XXI

Conversations with Josephine, Joseph, Joanna, Jonathan, Josie and Jolyon

The sayings quoted below are culled from a number of families, including my own. Some are adoptive families and some biological. All the conversations are genuine and none are touched up. All Nannies and *au pair* girls are referred to as "Val".

The ages ascribed to the children are pretty accurate as a note was usually made of the conversations within a day or two. Thus, obviously, the sayings are *not* "typical": had they been so, they would probably have been taken for granted by the listener and left unrecorded. They were noted because they were amusing or touching, or memorable for other reasons. Nevertheless I feel that, presented as they are in chronological order, they may reflect some of the predominant interests of children at different ages and also tell us something of the process of mental development, such as its spreading, fan-like shape.

Two–Three years

Early humour

Jolyon had had his water-play in the bath and was being dried by Mother. Josie was still "swimming" in the bath. M. to Jol: "There – are you dry now?" Jol: "Yes, I dry. Josie *wet* – Josie *naughty* girl!" Roars of laughter from two-year-old Jolyon at his own joke.

Generalising from one meaning of a word

Joanna, speaking with her mouth full, asked for more milk. M: "Swallow first . . . Now, have you finished?" Jo: "Bin", i.e. "been" – which is what she says when she has finished with the potty.

Organisation

M. and Jo enter bathroom, about to embark on ritual teeth-cleaning. Jo: "You turn on tap, I put in plug."

Observation

Two-and-a-half-year-old Jonathan, being introduced to his new baby sister, in the bath. M: "What do you think of her?" Jo: "Not much. She can't talk and she hasn't got a pom-pom."

Three-year-old Josephine, on first meeting her baby brother. "Oh, I didn't want one like that." "Why, what kind *did* you want?" "I wanted a black one."

This is a good indication of the (pernicious)role of *social learning* in acquiring colour-prejudice.

Early verbal invention

M: "Half-past seven – it's bed-time." Jo: "I'm going to – *not*-bed." A kind of junior partner of *Not The 9 O'clock News*.

After a two-hour drive, the family arrived at the coast. M. led Josephine behind a rock, took down her pants and asked her to do wee-wee. Josie obediently squatted down but, after a few ineffectual seconds, she announced, "It's shut!"

In an overcrowded lift in the underground, Jolyon suddenly proclaimed: "I mustn't do a 'whizzy' on all these people."

The conversations become less Rabelaisian as children grow older. However, some – like the first in the next section – are explicitly oedipal.

Three–Four years

Jonathan to his mother, out of the blue: "When I'm grown-up, I shall sleep with you." On another occasion, M: "Well, *I'm* going to bed." Jonathan: "Without Daddy?"

Reducing the novel to the familiar

Joanna, holidaying at the seaside, on meeting lady with three plump pekinese dogs – "Oh, *chickens!*"

Jolyon, *re* a visitor with a beard (unusual among his acquaintances): "I didn't like him at first but, when he came and said 'What's that, Jo?' and I said 'a camel' – then I did."

Reflections on the English language

After lunch, everyone usually gets a sweet – Mother, Val, Joanna and Joseph. Seeing that the tin contains only two sweets today, Jo says: "There are no left ones."

A visitor suggested that Josie should be painted. Her reaction: "But you don't paint *people!*"

Mrs Prunus lives with her husband and two grown-up sons. Next door lives three-year-old Joanna, who says one day to Mrs Prunus: "Have you got three men living with you?"

Later verbal invention

Jo: "I'm going to give a purple lecture" . . . (of Mr Gilbert) "I call him Mr Gilpotato" . . . (of a bottle-opener) "Is that an open-tinner?"

M: "What did you say?" Jo: "I'm not talking to you, I'm talking to myself." . . . "Oh, Mummy, I saw a horse pulling a horse-driver!"

Natural history and oceanography

Jo: "Where does the loo-water go when you pull the chain?" M: "Down to the sea." Jo: "What do the fishes do with the paper?"

Jo was curious about drains and drainage. In the bath one day he pulled out the plug before bath-time was over. M: "??" Jo: "I was only filling up the sea."

Quick on the draw

Joanna playing in garden with neighbour, Jolyon. Quarrel arises over what game to play. Joanna wants Mothers and Fathers and Jolyon wants Cowboys and Indians. M. asserts priority of guest. Some time later M. looks out of the window and sees Jolyon tied to a tree. She calls out: "But Joanna, I thought you were going to play Cowboys & Indians." Joanna: "Yes we are. Jolyon's my horse."

One night M. heard Jo cry out in his sleep. She went in and hugged him, whereupon he woke up and said, "I had a naughty think." M: "Oh, a bad dream?"

The interest in that particular conversation lies in the light it sheds on the acquisition of words denoting highly subjective concepts, such as DREAM. "A naughty think" is the closest that a three-and-a-half-year-old can get to expressing the experience of a nightmare.

First steps in philosophy

Shortly before dusk, Jo – after seeing a horse in a field: "Does the horse get dark?"

Advanced steps in philosophy

Jo: "My leg's my leg, my tummy's my tummy, my head's my head, but what is *me?*"

Jonathan, to his father: "Who will look after me when you and mother are dead?"

Early psychological observations

After twirling round and round the pillar on the porch, Joanna put her head into the house, and said: "Did you know the outside is going round and round?"

On being congratulated on having been a very good girl (she had been to a children's party with no contemporary for her), she replied: "And tomorrow I shall be *very bad*."

Having been reminded how she had fallen into a puddle last time she had disregarded advice, Joanna said: "Yes, and *you* were very sorry!"

Three to four is a good age for expressing uninhibited anger at adults. The child has acquired some measure of articulateness by this time but has not yet learned to repress the overt expression of anger. Thus Jo: "I'll throw you to the lions! . . . I'll give you puddle-water!"

In a shop, when Jo picked up some fragile object, the following conversation took place. Shop-keeper: "Don't do that, sonny." Jo hits shop-keeper. M: "Jo, you mustn't do that." Jo: "Well then, I'll spit!" M: "Oh, no, no." Jo: "Well then I'll fetch a policeman." Shop-keeper: "But the policeman's my friend." Jo: "Well, I'll bash this chair up!"

Four–Five years

Loyalty and identification with someone else

Scene: a children's party given by Josiah's parents, in honour of his fifth birthday. Playing Blind Man's Buff, Jolyon's mother was caught and was about to have her eyes bandaged. Jolyon shouted, "No! My Mummy's *not* funny!" and he flung his arms round his mother to stop her. (He also refused to be the Blind Man, himself.)

Future wife and Mum

Josie, observing chair-cover, badly scratched by cat: "That chair needs mending. I fetch my sewing" (which she duly did – and made a passable job of mending the cover).

Realising the implications of cooked meat
While eating rabbit for lunch, Jo suddenly remarked: "Rabbit is made from rabbit".

Further reflections on the English language
Again at lunch (but a different family). Jo: "I'd like a sheet of ham, please."

Having listened to a song, 'I'll go and court her for her beauty', Joanna: "Why does it say CAUGHT and not CATCH?"

Neighbour: "you must be specially kind to your mother, you know, because she's expecting a baby." Joseph: "But *I'm* expecting a baby too!"

Planning for the future
Jo: "When I'm grown up, I'm going to marry my John [his best friend] . . . and drive that crane what's at nursery school . . . I'm going to America over the sea . . . I'm going to Germany for ten weeks . . . My John likes you very much, Mummy."

Dawn of chivalry and concern for others
On a hilly country walk, with friends, Jo suddenly runs back, saying, "Are we going too quickly for you, Mummy? – Shall I help you, it's rather slippery here."

Joanna and Jonathan playing hospitals. She lies on the divan, covered in cushions, saying repeatedly to Jonathan: "Please, Doctor, serve me now . . . You must serve me. Say 'next please'." Jonathan, absorbed in his tractor, "I've only got one pair of hands," M. laughs. Jon: "That's what Val says."

At this age the struggle between truth, logic and emotion is sometimes transparently clear, as in the following conversation. Jolyon's father came up to say goodnight to his son and found the sheets bedaubed with lipstick. F: "Look what you've done to the sheets!" Jo: "No I haven't!" F: "But yes, you did!" Jo: "No, I *didn't!*" F: "Look, Jo, I won't be cross but I just want you to tell me the truth." Jo, after a pause, "Well I didn't do it – but I think I must have."

On the other hand, in less emotionally laden situations, young children can be ruthlessly logical, as shown in the following exchange between two five-year-olds. Joanna: "I saw a lorry." Joseph: "Oh, I didn't." Joanna: "It was a removal lorry." Joseph: "No it wasn't." Jan:

"Yes it was." Joseph: "Was it a big lorry or a little one?" Jan: "A little one." Joseph: "Then it wasn't a removal lorry."

The following illustrates practical application of the deductive method. A toy arrived by post, at Christmas: a bubble-blowing monkey, worked by electricity – but it did not work. Batteries run down ? Jo: "Let's get the tractor batteries and see if they're the same size."

Several children playing with a knarled old tree-trunk, in the woods. Jolyon: "It's a tractor." Josie: "Yes, I'm the guard." Jolyon: "No, guards don't be on tractors. You can be the conductor."

Joanna: "Waspses come only in the summer?" M: "Yes." Joanna: "Where they go in the winter?"

At tea-time, Jonathan and Josephine declaring that one should always take the nearest biscuit or cake. Jon, finally, "I shall take the biggest" (of the home-made cakes). Later M. hands him the plate so that the nearest is also the biggest. Jon takes it, saying, "I took the biggest." M: "and also the nearest." Jon, gazing gravely at M: *Thank you.*"

Generalisation; and self-criticism
Joanna, when asked by Val to hurry up with some domestic job, "I've only got one pair of feet" . . . Later, having made two contradictory statements, she says to herself, "I must make up my mind."

One way of putting it
Driving Josie and Jolyon through Cambridge, M. said: "That's Jesus College." Josie: "Oh, we've got a Jesus at school."

Imagination
Jon, Jan and M. having high tea in a café. Jon, surveying tomato sauce on his white plate: "Look, Mum, the plate's bleeding!"

Cart before horse? Or egg before hen?
When M. said goodnight to Jolyon's teddy-bear, after she had kissed Jo goodnight, he whispered, "They can't hear you 'cos they can't talk."

Thought in advance of language
Jo had diarrhoea one day. Asked how he felt, he said: "I have a little pain here and my bone is on the skin."

Ritual on Sunday walk

Jonathan and Josie were adopted siblings (unrelated by blood), separated in age by about a year. For many weeks, when out walking with their mother, Jon, aged four and a half, would go through the following routine: "I'm a baby tiger and my Mummy has died. Can I come and live with you?" M: "Yes, certainly, but I already have a son, called Jonathan." Jon: "Oh, he has died. *I'm* going to be your son now ... I have a baby sister too, a tigress in the jungle. Can she come and live with you too?" M: "Yes, certainly, but I already have a daughter called Josie" ... etc.

I do not fully understand the significance of this routine. Presumably it has to do with the fact of adoption and some need for reassurance.

Five–Six years

The first five remarks in this section illustrate developing philosophical preoccupations, some with a mathematical flavour

Jo – after having counted to over a hundred – "What comes after a million?"

M., at tea-time: "I don't want any more." Jo: "But you haven't had any."

The pudding was jam tart and all four of the lunchers wanted a second slice. Jo: "That will mean three cuts." M: "Yes." Jo: "It's interesting, isn't it, three cuts for four slices?"

Jo, walking in heavy snow with his mother, suddenly said: "Every place is somewhere." M: "How do you mean?" Jo: "Well, there's always a place wherever you go, isn't there? – And what happens after that ?"

Shortly after starting school, Jo: "If God made the world, where was he when he did it?"

The next seven show increasing interest and understanding of matters psychological

Jo (out of the blue): "You can't laugh when people hurts."

Joseph, after having expressed a wish to bang his baby sister: "What makes people do things – laugh or cry or be nasty?"

Jolyon had made an enormous stain on his table napkin. M: "Oh, your poor table napkin!" Jol, scornfully: "Napkins can't *feel*."

At another meal, Joanna: "We're having strawberries for pudding." Guest: "That's probably a secret." Joseph: "Well, you can forget it, can't you? ... He helped himself to two jelly babies, one black and

196

one orange, saying: "I shall eat the black one first because I don't like the colour of black but I do like the taste of black."

Josephine, after reporting that she had known something that the others in her class didn't know: "But that's really because you're such a good mother."

Jo, on getting into the bath: "The water's very hot – oh, perhaps it's only because *I'm* very *cold*".

Religious concern is apt to appear at this stage, probably owing to school influence
Joseph and house-guest folding sheets together. Guest: "You fold sheets very well. Did Val teach you?" Joseph: "No, God taught me. He's a very wonderful man, you know."

When Jo went to stay with ex-Nanny Val, he asked Val's mother if God was living. The reply is unrecorded but I think twenty-one-year-old Val's comment is worth noting. She said curtly: "He ought to ask a clergyman."

Josie: "Do I really *have* to go to Heaven?" Having been reassured that this was by no means certain on any count, she asked, "But are there really *lobsters* there?" It later transpired that her teacher had taken the nippers of a lobster to show the class, and when a child had asked her, "But where's the rest of the lobster, is it in Heaven?" had replied that it was.

Looking towards the future
Jo: "I think I shall have to be a bus driver because it must be so awfully difficult to keep the train on the rails if you're an engine driver. The engine has no steering wheel."

Josephine was ill in bed. When asked next day how she was, she answered: "I'm a little bit all right."

Looking through an old album with the children, M. showed photographs of her mother and father. Jo asked: "Where are you?" M: "Oh, this was before I was born." Jo: "Don't be silly, Mummy, who would have looked after us?"

That is an excellent example of the difficulty experienced by a young child in grasping the earlier non-existence of himself or his intimates.

The section ends with a last instance of uninhibited anger and momentary hatred (probably far less damaging to the child than repressed and unrecognised anger). Jonathan five and a half and Joseph seven and a half are brothers. After some discussion about

197

which should go to bed first that evening, their father says they will toss for it. The penny is tossed and Jonathan loses. Jon to F: "You like Joseph best." F: "No, that's not true." Jon: "Well, then, you wish I were dead." F: "No, I don't, Jonathan." Jon: "Well, I shall kill you!"

Six–Seven years

On her first flight, as the aircraft took off, Josie turned to her mother and said, "And shall we really get quite small now?"

At this age, Jolyon often asked how the world began. Last time, however, he added, "But I think it's so nice that there *is* a world!"

After having played a major scale very evenly, he said, "It's just like a heart-beat, isn't it?"

Jonathan read the page number (116) of the last chapter in his book correctly, but then added, grinning, "It looks like eleventy-six, doesn't it?"

Jo, having been introduced to April Fool's Day: "Isn't it lovely to have a day in the year when you can say what *isn't* true and what is funny?"

Practising arithmetical tables. M: "Three *whats* are eighteen?" Jo: "Three *whats* – three WATTS – what a tiny light!"

Seven–Eight years

An older friend had tightened up Jo's bicycle basket so that it no longer rattled as she rode. Jo, having thanked him, asked, "Did you take the bike off?"

M. was washing Jolyon's neck. Jo: "It hurts when you wash my neck." M: "In ten years time you'll be taking out some lovely lady and you'll take great trouble to have a clean neck." Jo: "Oh no, Mum, when I grow up I shall marry someone quite ordinary, like you."

Alchemy?
A propos of changing money on projected holiday abroad, Jo: "Do they let you watch them while they change it?"

Jo, gazing at lighthouse, far away on the mole: "It's funny, that lighthouse is smaller than my thumb – but it isn't *really*".

While reading a Ladybird book about Nelson, he commented: "A *French* boy might not enjoy reading this so much."

Joseph kept advising Joanna, while she was playing (the boardgame) Fox & Geese with M. M. to Joe: "Please don't, Jo – *I'll* give advice if necessary." Joe: "It's rather difficult to supervise someone's game when you're playing against them, isn't it?"

The next (and last) remark in this section is included because it is moving in its tenderness and understanding – and it is also of particular interest since the Jonathan in question is now a paediatrician. Aged eight and a half, he entered the room where his mother was breast-feeding his baby sister and said: "It makes me feel quite sad to see you feeding her because *I* shall never be able to feed a baby."

I shall call a halt here because after eight years of age children say memorable things so frequently that recording becomes a difficult task, and selecting from notes becomes even more arbitrary. Let us end the chapter with one Jonathan remark, made at the age of ten, and two from Joanna, at twelve years of age.

Val having accidentally broken a wine-glass, M. commented: "Well, I don't mind all that much. I mind much more about *living* things than inanimate things." Jon: "Yes. *Books* are almost like animate things, aren't they?"

This is interesting on three counts. It illustrates a ten-year-old's love of reading; it shows his awareness of the power of books to *communicate*; and it suggests, too, awareness that the distinction between animate and inanimate is perhaps one of degree rather than kind.

The following two comments from Joanna, at twelve, are deserving of mention, the first because of the curiosity expressed (in a habitually unreflective child) and the second because it is so hilarious. Moreover the two jointly illustrate the fascinating blend of sophistication and naïvety that are characteristic of this age. It thus forms a good lead-in to the chapter on Adolescence.

Joanna: "Are you unconscious when you're asleep?"

and, later,

"If Prince Charles marries me, you'll be the Queen Mother, won't you – and Jonathan will be King Jonathan."

XXII
Adolescence

> Not yet old enough for a man, nor young enough for a boy; as a squash is
> before 'tis a peascod, or a codling, when 'tis almost an apple: 'tis with him
> in standing water, between boy and man.
>
> *Twelfth Night*, I.v, Malvolio to Olivia.

Malvolio's description of an adolescent male (which is how he
perceives Viola, dressed as Cesario) is apt and vivid. I paused
momentarily over the phrase "in standing water" – since that image
sounded too static for the notorious restlessness of adolescence – but
I then observed a kindly note at the bottom of the page, informing me
that the phrase in question signifies "when the tide is turning",
whereupon I understood. The sea is indeed restless at that time,
apparently uncertain whether it is coming or going, very much as the
adolescent appears to his elders and – if one may trust to reminiscence
– how one frequently felt, oneself, as a teenager.

The adolescent is both a child and an adult, possessing many of the
urges and the physical capacities of the latter while still retaining the
impatience, intolerance and inexperience of the former. Growing up
consists in acquiring the patience, toleration and wisdom that stem
from experience, and enabling the various conflicting human traits to
coexist harmoniously in the one frame (at least in theory).

The period of adolescence may be equated, roughly, with the
period from twelve to eighteen years of age. But the physical signs of
puberty sometimes start as young as ten or eleven – and the various
mental and physiological changes tend to arouse, and repercuss on,
one another. This is partly because the older generation begins
treating the developing individual in a different way and, throughout

200

life, one tends to behave (to some extent, even to become) as one is treated. Jonathan is acutely conscious of the down appearing on his face, the occasional uncontrollability of his voice and the fact that his shoulders are suddenly too broad for his favourite jacket; and Joanna is equally conscious of her burgeoning bosom – accentuating, as it does, her slimming waist – and the insidious growth of her body-hair.

It is up to Jo's parents to determine whether this awareness is to become a sheepish, uncomfortable self-consciousness or, on the contrary, to become a source of eager, forward-looking pride. The latter is infinitely preferable – not only for Jo's serenity and peace of mind, but also because, if he is helped to find the accelerating process of growing-up to be pleasurable, he will welcome it and go along with it. If, on the other hand, he is constantly teased, criticised and thwarted, he is liable to become withdrawn or hostile and unco-operative.

This counsel, however, is more easily given than followed. There is plenty to disapprove of about Jo during these years. He may become aggressive and opinionated or secretive and sulky, awkward in manner, discourteous with his parents' friends, touchy about even the gentlest criticism. There is often a lot of door-slamming at this stage. The same may well apply to Joanna; in addition, she may indulge in infuriating, baffling fits of prolonged giggling with her contemporaries and develop strange tastes in make-up and clothes.

Not all teenagers radically change their personality: some take things more calmly (though *their* change of style may develop later) and a few seem positively to improve – which tends to mean, in this context, that they begin to conform more closely to their parents' norms! However adolescence affects Jo, the wisest strategy is not to over-react and not to panic. The latency period – seen in retrospect, perhaps, as a honeymoon period – is now over and it is natural that psychological changes should accompany physical development.

Hitherto, Jo may cheerfully have left to you choice of hairstyle, television programmes, food preferences, pastimes, clothes and – to some extent – friendships and reading habits, if any. In adolescence, however, his attitude to many of these may drastically alter. In the first place, he may find it imperative to *discover for himself* a new barber, fresh programmes, different foods, etc. Secondly, he may believe that in all these areas the *more different* his new style, the *better*. For a time he finds his parents' ideas old-fashioned, their tastes dull and their values derisory.

It may well be only "for a time". My Jo used sometimes to say

201

scornfully (as when I had painstakingly acquired some ultra-bright yellow socks for him – which I did not particularly care for) "Oh, that was just a phase"; and more than once, in reply to a remonstrance from me, he replied, would-be consolingly, "It's probably just a phase, Mother." Sometimes it was, and sometimes it wasn't – but it is courting trouble for *a parent* to designate any of Jo's behaviour as "just a phase". He also said, in all seriousness: "I can take criticism from some people, but not from you." And, in lighter vein, "I may be rebellious but I'm not revolting!" And – very pertinent to this chapter – "You can't learn from other people's experience."

This is perhaps the master-key to "the problem of adolescence". The teenager does not wish to learn from the experience of others: hence, he does not believe it is possible to do so -- and, *without* such belief, it is indeed impossible. Not all are equally explicit on the subject, but many feel an intense desire to try things out for themselves – whether it is smoking, alcohol (in excess – or other drugs), sex, spiky green hair, some form of mysticism, shop-lifting, safety-pins in the ear or travel abroad. Most conventional parents are against such innovations, with the exception of travel – to which we shall return in the next chapter.

The best parental policy is, I think, to present to Jo the dangers – if dangers there be – in such courses of action. The presentation should be quiet, objective, factual – not highly dramatised and overbearing or dogmatic. Thus if the issue is, for instance, smoking, do not concentrate too much on the risk to Jo's health. This may be your main objection (whether or not you, yourself, smoke) but it will carry little weight with Jo. In the teens, the "won't happen to me" attitude is particularly strong and interestingly enough it extends, in some adolescents, even to death and to old age.

My Joanna volunteered to me, when she was about eleven, "I shall never be forty" – and she was certainly not envisaging an early demise. Her imagination simply would not rise to the notion of her ever being anything but young. So, having mentioned the health hazards of smoking – which will already be familiar to Jo – discuss with him, rather, the discomfort caused to others, the expense and the difficulty of dropping the habit once it is established.

Similarly with drugs: point out the loss of personal freedom that drug-taking engenders and the way in which it impinges on, and interferes with, other pursuits. Jo may appear unyielding during such discussions – in which event do not insist. But in course of time you may surprisingly find that the talk has had some effect and that Jo is

202

taking your advice to heart – especially if he can do so without loss of face.

The practice of taking drugs such as heroin or marijuana, prevalent in the 1960s and early 1970s, seems to have declined of recent years, at least temporarily. But other drugs are abused in their place: some are sniffed, some injected, some smoked and some are swallowed. If these practices are popular among Jo's friends, it may be quite hard for him to steer clear of them. He may "try it just once, to see what it's like" and, indeed, never touch it again – either because he does not enjoy it first time or because, he realises, he enjoys it too much. On the other hand it is sadly easy to get "hooked" and then Jo will need your help, for his friends and acquaintances will mostly be pushing one way – to say nothing of the persistent "pushers" themselves. The latters' whole way of life depends on their retaining their present slaves and gaining more addicts.

Alert parents may spot suggestive symptoms at an early stage: eye-pupils may become unusually large or small, speech may become slurred or otherwise altered, an unusual odour may emanate from Jo and he may become more secretive in his habits. If in doubt, seek skilled advice. Your doctor should be able to confirm or refute your fears and, if a fairly late stage has been reached, he will let you know of a suitable drug-addiction centre where Jo could go for treatment. It is, in general, the inadequate or the depressed teenager for whom drugs are more than a passing phase and who is silently crying out for adult assistance.

The problem of drinking to excess, however, is ever-prevalent, some – though by no means all – future alcoholics getting addicted in late adolescence. Like many of the less desirable habits, this one is far easier to acquire than to drop. Some people – of all ages – drink to excess because they are unhappy or insecure, and they find that if they take sufficient alcohol the edges of their misery become comfortingly blurred (despite the ensuing horrors of the morning after and, eventually, of their shrunken purse and liver). Others between, say, seventeen and twenty-five go to the pub most evenings and drink with like-minded companions because they have no inner resources or major interests – and at this stage it is rather late to build up such interests. As they put it, "Life is so *boring* . . . there's nothing else to do . . . everybody does it . . ."

The last remark is perhaps the most significant. "Everybody does it", i.e. the people they associate with do it (far from everybody of their age, in fact); and there is also the unspoken assumption of pride – that it is dashing and virile to drink a lot, to be able to hold one's drink and to pay for the next round. (Some girls follow the same pattern, but this particular weakness is more characteristically masculine.)

The information that alcohol "provokes the desire but takes away the performance", as the Porter says in *Macbeth*, would be considered irrelevant by these young people – as would be the suggestion that the habit is ever-encroaching. "There's nothing wrong with social drinking in moderation," they may assert – rightly, in my view; "and we can reduce it or give it up quite easily, any time we want" – mistakenly claimed, quite often.

What prophylactic steps then can be taken to avoid this potentially tragic state of affairs? – in which the individual is "normal" only after he has had a few drinks. My recommendation is to let Jo have a little wine, or a little cider or sherry from an early age, when his parents and their friends are doing so, particularly with a meal. If he does not like it, do not force it on him but try again a year or two later. If he enjoys it from the beginning, keep his intake very low but gradually increase the amount, and the variety of drinks – until, at sixteen or seventeen, he is used to social drinking and takes it as a matter of course. If he does seem to be getting too fond of alcohol, explain the hazards of excess and point out to him the *childishness* of overdoing it and the loss of control and of freedom that follows. (Almost all late teenagers would rather be called vicious than childish.) Clearly, in these strong waters, no tactics are infallible; and, equally clearly, such a course will hardly commend itself to teetotallers.

In many cases, however, this approach works well, if taken in time. Needless to say, even if Jo is a moderate and a social drinker, it is worth discussing with him the ills attendant on drinking-and-driving. Apart from the legal aspect, the dangers *to others* should be emphasised. You may grant that Jo's own driving remains impeccable after a drink or two (yet mentioning the typical alcoholic illusion of over-confidence) but point out to him that – as all drivers will agree – an accident is invariably the other chap's fault!

What you feel about sexual experimentation will probably depend on your own sexual habits but it is, in any case, worth commenting on the dreary triviality of sex without mutual love and tenderness. In all such discussions, get Jo to do as much talking as possible and bear in mind the adage about people who live in glass houses.

In situations where your main objection is the immediate anxiety caused to you – as, for instance, by Joanna's not getting home until 2.00 a.m. – frankly explain your anxiety (as opposed to censuring her way of life) and try to effect a compromise by getting her to ring up if she realises she will be home later than midnight – or whatever time you suggest.

The posture that most annoys Jo at this time is the assumption of omniscience or of power on the part of parents. Admission of their own weakness, and acceptance of his existence as a separate human being and his rights as an emerging adult, are what he wants and needs – but this must not be mere lip-service, it must be genuinely felt. Adolescents (like children) are quick to recognise and despise any act put on for their benefit – if it is "just an act".

I do not wish to give the impression that the parent is always primarily to blame if things go wrong in adolescence, nor that the period is necessarily a "problem" period: I do not believe either of these propositions to be true. My reasons for writing as I have are that adolescence has long been perceived as a difficult time for all concerned, that many parents express a desire for counselling at this stage and, as may be recalled from certain passages in Part I, some feel that every succeeding generation of young people presents greater problems. I doubt also that this is the case. The problems of succeeding generations are *different* (owing for instance to the present availability of reliable contraceptives, the change in the age of reaching legal majority and the fact that more adolescents have more money and leisure than in the past – and, hence, they own motor-cycles, etc., at an earlier age), but the problems are not necessarily *graver*. Indeed, from some points of view, the technological advances and the spread of education for everybody up to the age of sixteen should, in theory, render a "good life" easier for all concerned.

This of course begs the vital question: what is meant by a "good life"? And, good for whom? – since the problem teenagers and the problem parents seem to feel that their requirements are incompatible. The reader who has doggedly read this far will know roughly what I consider to be the essentials of good living and how I think they can best be achieved. I believe that in babyhood and childhood a framework should be established which allows Jo a certain measure of freedom, once the habit of obedience and co-operation has been inculcated. The obedience should be neither blind nor resentful. After about five or six, Jo should be asked rather than commanded to behave in certain ways; he should come to realise *why* this behaviour is enjoined; and, if he thinks otherwise, he should express his opinion, confident that it will be respected, and discussed in friendly fashion.

As the latency period draws to its close, however, Jo should be granted greater freedom in all spheres. And by the time the end of adolescence approaches he should be treated as mature – and feel himself to be so – with the choices and the responsibilities of an adult. If he abuses this freedom – and, in particular, if such abuse causes distress or embarrassment to others – this is sad and his parents may feel a sense of failure. There is little point, however, in their taking him to task. If so doing has not worked in the past, it is unlikely to succeed at this late stage. On the contrary, it is liable to build up further barriers and, perhaps, to do lasting damage to the relationship. Let Jo see that the umbilical cord is irretrievably cut and he may even return to the fold, scattering mixed metaphors in his wake!

XXIII
The Young Adult

Since this book concerns the rearing of children, a chapter on the young adult may well be thought superfluous. It will indeed be short. I wish only to make three points: first to stress the importance of Jo's spending some time away from home; secondly, to impress on her parents that every family has its ups and downs, however it may appear to an outsider; and thirdly, to remind them that once Jo has reached years of discretion, it is too late to do anything about her development and, therefore, that they should stop worrying and settle down to enjoy the pleasures of her life at a distance. Give advice or help only if she requests it.

In Chapter XXII I briefly mentioned travel abroad. I did not pursue the topic there as I was dealing mainly with activities viewed by most parents with dismay, and the normal parent – insofar as such exists – will be delighted if Jo wishes to spread her wings and acquaint herself with new places and people. "Normal" or not, Jo's parents should welcome the prospect and, if Jo herself does not propose leaving home for a time, they should take the initiative.

I say "travel abroad", that is, out of the country. Most young people enjoy this experience and gain a great deal from it. Jo and her companions will learn at first-hand that different lands have different customs: this prompts them to recognise and question for the first time much that they have taken for granted in their home-country. Jo will learn also that "foreigners" are not an alien species but are as human as she is – and she will gain perspective as she comes to realise that, when abroad *she* is the "foreigner". She will come to appreciate the problems of making herself understood in an unfamiliar language, and this will give her insight into the difficulties encountered by visitors to her own country (and also to young children). Incidentally, coming to grips with a new language will teach her a lot about the English tongue. Most crucial, she will acquire the ability to stand on her own feet, away from the amenities and supervision of home.

This is a vital part of growing up. To learn this Jo need not, of course, go abroad, and she need not – indeed she *should not* – wait until she is fully adult. It is an excellent idea for parents to send Jo away for a week or two – to relatives or friends or camp – from the time she reaches double figures. After this, the length of time away, and the distance from home, may be extended. She should go away at least once a year. If Jo enjoys these visits from the beginning, well and good (and, parents, do guard against uttering reproachful cries of, "Didn't you miss us at all?") If, however, Jo is very homesick on the first visit, this shows how essential these trips are for her – and she will probably settle down better on subsequent occasions.

I have come across a number of instances of young men and women in their late teens whose first experience of being away from home was as university students – and they could not endure it. They telephoned home every day; they went home every weekend; and in several cases they gave up the struggle, relinquishing their hard-won university place to live at home, apron-strung and apologetic for the next few years. In one case, to my knowledge, the experience of missing home was so shattering, and the sense of failure so intense, that the young man committed suicide.

Thus learning to live away from home is an absolute must and should be begun fairly early in life, and taken in easy stages. And if, in late adolescence or early adulthood, Jo expresses the desire to travel abroad – on her own or with a friend or two – she should be warmly encouraged to do so.

My second point is that some parents gain the impression that other people's families are ideal and trouble-free – *all the time*. The Field-Maples, for instance, honestly believe that all members of the Hornbeam household have permanently equable and sunny temperaments, that there is no quarrelling or grumbling in the family, no educational or vocational problems, and that the house is always admirably clean and orderly. They would be incredulous if told that the Hornbeams regard the Field-Maples with equal envy! In my experience these wholly fortunate, trouble-free families do not exist. Some have more vicissitudes than others, admittedly; and some make heavier weather of their troubles than others.

The reason I raise the issue is that the Field-Maples, who have had their share of problems recently, become even more depressed when they consider the Hornbeams (*and* the Osiers). They sometimes feel that they have been selected, in a unique and Job-like way, to suffer more than their share of misfortunes. Illogical though it may be, the knowledge that others – that almost everyone else – is in a similar if not identical boat, is curiously comforting.

Finally, Jo is now grown-up. She has left school, is legally of age and has decided what she wants to do. Her character, manners and way-of-life are now determined. Her parents have done their best and they should now "let go" – for Jo's sake as well as their own. In course of time *they* may be seeking advice from *her*. Whatever the present situation, and whatever lies ahead, there is much to enjoy. There is reason to go on living, there is a future consisting of an intriguing, large question-mark.

Selected References

Adoption

Clarke, A.M. & Clarke, A.D.B., *Early Experience: Myth and Evidence*, Open Books, 1976.
Humphrey, Michael, *The Hostage Seekers*, Longman, 1969,
Kornitzer, Margaret, *Adoption and Family Life*, Putnam, 1968.
McWhinnie, A.M., *Adopted Children – How They Grow Up*, Routledge & Kegan Paul, 1967.
Maxwell, Vicky, *The Chosen Child*, Collins, 1973.
Tizard, Barbara, *Adoption: A Second Chance*, Open Books, 1977.

The Facts of Life

For Four–Eight-year-olds:
Hegeler, Stan, *Peter & Caroline,* Tavistock Publications, 1957 (1976, 9th Impression).
For Ten–Eleven-year-olds:
Pilkington, Roger, *The Facts of Life for Children*, British Medical Association.
For Nine–Twelve-year-olds:
Kenner, Jill, *Where Do Babies Come From?* National Marriage Guidance Council.
For Teenagers:
Delarge, B. & Emin, D., *Girls Growing Up*, Geoffrey Chapman, 1972.
Delarge, B. edited and adapted by Wallace, Margaret, *Boys Growing Up*, Geoffrey Chapman, 1971.
Pilkington, Roger, *Who's Who And Why*, Delisle.

For Parents:

Delarge, B. and Emin, D., *Girls Growing Up, Parents' Book: The Sexual Education of Pre-Adolescent Girls*, Geoffrey Chapman, 1969.

Wallace, Margaret, *Let There Be Jo: a young child talks with mother about how babies begin*, Geoffrey Chapman, 1971.

Wallace, Margaret, *For Parents of Boys Growing Up: The Sexual Education of Pre-Adolescent Boys*, Geoffrey Chapman, 1972.

General

Gibbens, John, *The Case of Young Babies*, J. & A. Churchill, 1955.

Gibbens, John, *The Care Of Children From One To Five Years*, Association of Maternity & Child Welfare Centres, 1936.

Leach, Penelope, *Babyhood*, Penguin, 1974.

Leach, Penelope, *Baby & Child*, Michael Joseph, 1977, Penguin, 1980.